Professional Careers by Design

A Handbook for the Bespoke Life

Sharon K. Hull, MD, MPH

ADVANCE PRAISE FROM READERS FOR PROFESSIONAL CAREERS BY DESIGN™: A HANDBOOK FOR THE BESPOKE LIFE

In a book that is both inspirational and practical, Sharon Hull brings design thinking to career planning. It is clear why Hull has the outstanding coaching reputation that she enjoys. This book engages the reader's mind and heart through challenging questions, reflective exercises, and pertinent examples. It is poised to become an important tool that aspiring and established leaders can use throughout their career.

Lois Margaret Nora, MD, JD, MBA, President Emeritus, Northeastern Ohio Medical University; President, Medical School Advisory Group.

With today's uncertainty in jobs and specialties which are compounded by changing economy and a pandemic changing how things are done and what working looks like, many are looking at their careers and wondering where they are and where they want to go and should they go. There are also new individuals entering the workforce who are just getting started in their careers wondering where they will wander over their career. There are likely few in the workforce that aren't asking questions. What if you could have a coach in your back pocket? One that could ask you key questions, get you to reach into your inner self and find the answers that are best for you at any time in your career? Dr. Hull's book Professional Careers by Design™: A Handbook for the Bespoke Life can serve as that coach and point you in the direction that you want to go now and help you reassess as your career moves along and the next curve is on the horizon.

Betsy Ripley, MD, Professor of Medicine and Senior Associate Dean for Faculty Affairs, Virginia Commonwealth University School of Medicine.

Hull's Professional Careers by Design™: A Handbook for the Bespoke Life is the ultimate roadmap for professionals who are navigating their way through each phase of their career. Drawing from her experience as a medical professional and academic as well as her years coaching clients, Hull has crafted a methodology supported to the brim with resources, templates, tools, and her hallmark thought-provoking questions. This is the next best thing to working with her one-on-one as her voice carefully, skillfully and strategically nudges you along your personal journey towards crafting the ideal professional career.

Debbie Lawrence, Leadership and Business Coach, Founder and President, Abundant Living Inc.

Professional Careers by Design™: A Handbook for the Bespoke Life has utility for professionals in the 21st century at every career stage. Whether you are beginning your first day or leaving your retirement party, this wonderfully written book provides sage advice and thought-provoking questions to help you successfully navigate your first, second, and third acts as a professional. Dr. Hull is a gifted writer and clear-eyed thinker who draws upon her deep reservoir of experience as a physician, educator, and executive coach to gently but firmly guide readers to pay attention to themselves and their environments and to make proactive decisions that align personal and professional goals.

Bettina M. Beech, DrPH, MPH, Clinical Professor of Population Health and Chief Population Health Officer, University of Houston

As the leader of a national faculty development fellowship program, I see the immediate applicability of this book. Faculty and their departments are all better served by professionals who successfully curate the career they want rather than endure the career that is available. Personally, I can't wait to work with the Mid-Career Awakening chapter. So many fields are experiencing the brain drain caused by Boomers' mass retirement. Sooner than they realize, mid-career faculty will find themselves playing the role of Senior Expert or Wise Elder. This content will help them manage that transition.

Thomas F. Koonce, MD, MPH, Associate Professor and Vice Chair of Education, Department of Family Medicine; Director, UNC Family Medicine Faculty Development Fellowship; Associate Chief Medical Officer for Outpatient Services, University of North Carolina School of Medicine

The Professional Careers by Design™ Model

Discernment

Managing Change

Lifelong Context

What Matters Most to You?

The Career Transitions Cycle

The Life Course of a Career

To Cindy Fraed, who not only tolerated but celebrated the time I spent writing this book, and who believed in this work before I even knew it existed: my deepest gratitude. I could not have done it without you.

And to my constant companion, Sophie, who was always by my side as I learned how to be a coach and as I figured out what to write about and when the time had come to do so: you were truly Joy Wrapped in Fur. Thank you for that gift. May I embody and inhabit your joy!

Professional Careers by Design

A Handbook for the Bespoke Life

Sharon K. Hull, MD, MPH

Published by Metta Solutions, LLC

Durham, NC

2023

LIST OF FIGURES

LIST OF TOOLS

Tools for Discernment

Tools for Managing Transitions

Tools for Lifelong Context

CONTENTS

Part 4: Lifelong Context – Development Along the Life Course

FOREWORD

Now, more than ever, professional coaching is a critical tool in the development of a successful and meaningful career. I know this is true, because as the senior vice dean for faculty at Drexel University College of Medicine and the executive director of Executive Leadership in Academic Medicine® (ELAM), the nation's only longitudinal leadership program for women in academic medicine, dentistry, public health and pharmacy, and our new program, Executive Leadership in Health Care (ELH), for women executives in hospitals and health care systems, I have counseled hundreds of leaders as they have prepared to make significant transitions in their careers.

When an already strained American health care system was pummeled by the impact of COVID-19—resulting in profound burnout among clinicians, providers, and leaders—disruption set the stage for mass re-evaluation of what these and professionals in myriad other fields wanted from their careers and their lives. As we all emerged from this crisis, I spoke with countless colleagues who want more—or different—focal points in their careers.

One of the most important resources we can offer colleagues who are in distress, hungering for a significant change in their career, or simply striving to be the most effective and influential they can be in their current role, is professional coaching. As an early adopter of what the business world clearly knew was an effective resource for supporting leadership growth, ELAM has always embraced the value of coaching, incorporating coaching into its curriculum for fellows and as a vital and ongoing support system after completion of the program. As an integral part of the ELAM program, where she leads our coaching efforts, Dr. Sharon Hull has been committed to elevating coaching and designing new ways to provide this support to our network and beyond. In Professional Careers by Design™: A Handbook for the Bespoke Life, she gives you access to many of the key coaching principles and processes that countless leaders have relied on.

This book offers a distillation of what it means to design a career that is meaningful to you, purposeful and intentional. Her step-by-step instructions and opportunities to reflect and engage through immersive exercises provide tangible ways to tackle what might feel like an overwhelming task — redesigning your future, so that you can align your personal and professional goals.

I congratulate you for taking charge of your next steps. I wish you all the best as you sculpt your career and your life into exactly what you envision.

Nancy D. Spector, MD

Professor of Pediatrics
Betty A. Cohen Chair in Women's Health
Senior Vice Dean for Faculty
Executive Director, Lynn Yeakel Institute for Women's
  Health and Leadership (IWHL)
Executive Director, Executive Leadership in Academic Medicine® (ELAM)
  and Executive Leadership in Health Care
Drexel University College of Medicine

ACKNOWLEDGMENTS

I owe a debt of gratitude to so many people for their support and contributions to the creation of this work. An author always worries about leaving someone out and strives to provide a complete list. I hope I have done so here. So many thanks to all of you.

- To my wife, Cindy, thank you for believing in and supporting me in getting this work out into the world. You have been my confidant, my sounding board, my encourager, my first reader, my proofreader, and my cheerleader at every step of the way. Namaste.

- To Cathie Siders, who invited me to my own Encore Career, you have my deepest respect and gratitude for all the ways you have played a part in my journey.

- To Melissa Turner, who has lived with my voice in her head helping write the Metta Solutions Blog, our newsletter, and many other things along the way, thank you for your extensive edits and overall contributions to this work. They are many and I am grateful!

- To Debbie Lawrence, my dear friend and co-traveler on the journey of "entrepreneurship with integrity," thank you for your steadfastness, your detailed feedback, and your friendship.

- To Raina Merchant, my biggest cheerleader for this project outside my own home, thank you for the persistent nudges to get this work out the door and into the world.

- To Lois Nora, for teaching me about leadership, about what matters most, and about taking good care of myself, I am grateful beyond measure.

- To Ann Brown, for creating opportunity and supporting my journey as a professional coach.

- To Jim Maurer, who coached me in the details and intricacies of publishing a book, thank you for all the time spent on the phone, reading manuscripts and proposals, and helping me find my way.

- To the Metta Solutions Team: Ashli Brown, Robin Gibbs, Martine Jackson, Mark Pandick and Melissa Turner. You have made possible this work of creativity. I am so grateful you are on this journey with me!

- To all my alpha and beta readers: Elizabeth Ripley, Bettina Beech, Mark Pandick, Mira Irons, Nancy Spector, Debbie Lawrence, Linda Sanders, David Flagel, Thomas Koonce, Raina Merchant, Cindy Fraed. Thank you all for feedback on the concepts, structure, and technical editing for this whole document. Your input made this a better book!

- To the faculty, staff, fellows, and alumnae of the Executive Leadership in Academic Medicine program at Drexel University, thank you for the opportunity to learn from and with you for many years.

- To my mother, Delores Hull, for teaching me to read, and to value the written word; and to my father, William Hull, for teaching me how to think critically about complex problems. To both my parents for their love and support throughout my lifetime, and for teaching me that how we treat each other matters.

INTRODUCTION

I have written this book after twelve years of professional executive coaching with individuals from many career paths. It represents the distillation of what I have learned from all of them, and I am most grateful for what they have taught me.

For you, the reader, I offer this bit of guidance about how to get the most out of the book. There are three components of the Professional Careers by Design™ approach:

- Discernment: What Matters Most to You

- Managing Change: The Career Transitions Cycle

- Lifelong Context: The Life Course of a Professional Career

Some of you will find value in reading the book cover to cover. Part 1 offers some basic concepts that will be useful as you think about designing your own career, and I encourage you to take the time to start with this section.

Some of you will realize that you are in the process of trying to figure out what matters to you about your personal and professional life and are trying to align your efforts with what matters. If this is you, read Part 1 and then move to the Discernment section (Part 2). It is likely that Parts 3 and 4 will be helpful now, or at some point in the future, so read them when you find them useful.

Some others among you are looking for a guide on how to manage a transition or change in your career, either by your own choosing or as a matter of circumstance. For you, starting with the Managing Change section (Part 3) may make the most sense, and you may find the guidance in the Discernment section (Part 2) will help you manage the change you are currently undergoing.

A different group of you may be at either the beginning or the culmination of your career, and you may find that the ability to understand the bigger perspective of your career in its long-term arc will help you make sense of what comes next. If you are a trainee in any profession, the Lifelong Context component (Part 4) may help you see the trajectory of your career in a different light than you have considered before. And, if you are at the peak of your senior career and wondering what to do for an encore, Part 4 may give you a perspective on what you have accomplished and what more you still want to give or do in the world.

The work of an intentionally designed professional career does not end when you land your dream job, or even when you retire (*if* you retire), nor are these principles limited to the professional areas of your life. As long as you choose to be intentional, there will always be work and reflection to be done.

That is why for many of my clients, the Professional Careers by Design™ approach is just the beginning of building what I call a "Bespoke Life," a life that in all its aspects (professional, spiritual, physical, intellectual, and every other dimension you can consider) serves what matters most to you and those for whom you care most. As you make these processes into lifelong habits, I invite you to consider how you could apply them broadly to craft an entire life that is uniquely yours and uniquely meaningful.

However you choose to approach this book, I hope you will take away the following message: **Creating a Bespoke Life — crafting it with intention, meaning, and purpose while doing good in the world — is a LIFELONG aspirational journey, and one that goes well beyond planning your path from one job to the next.**

This book is written to serve as your guide on that journey, one you can return to for help at every step of the way. But it's not the only support system you'll need. That's why I also hope that you will join *The Bespoke Life Book Club* in my free online community, *The Bespoke Life Network*, where you can learn and connect with others who are also striving to design more fulfilling, meaningful lives around the things that matter most to them. As part of the Book Club, you'll gain access to helpful tools and resources to support your progress, as well as a ready-made community of people who believe that we can make the world (and our own world) better by building a Bespoke Life that honors who we are and what we care about. More details on the benefits of the Book Club are provided in Chapter 24. You can join the *Bespoke Life Book Club* by using this QR code to sign up (membership in the Book Club is free).

Figure 1: QR Code to Enroll in the Bespoke Life Book Club

Thank you for taking the time to read this work. I wish you blessings for the journey.

Sharon Hull, MD, MPH

Walker, there is no road, the road is made by walking.[1]

~Antonio Machado~

PART 1

Professional Careers by Design – Crafting a Bespoke Career

What if I told you that there was a way to successfully navigate every career decision you will need to make over the course of your lifetime? And what if I told you that it's a straightforward (though not simple), portable, and repeatable process? Would you be interested? I would, and so would my coaching clients.

What I'm about to share with you is the distillation of my own experience in a thirty-five-year professional career, and my experience working with hundreds of professionals over thousands of hours as a professional executive coach. In my work, I specialize in helping people create what I call a Bespoke Life, working with people who want to positively impact the world, intentionally design lives of meaning and purpose, and create good in the world around them.

The word "bespoke" implies a custom-crafted approach, tailor-made to the individual. People who are intentional about what they want from life, both personally and professionally, are crafting their life to fit their values. To do this, people must align their personal and professional goals and values with the ways in which they spend their time. This book will help you achieve that alignment and be well on your way to crafting your own bespoke career and integrating it into a custom-crafted, bespoke life.

More than ever before, as the world recovers from the COVID-19 pandemic, our work lives are in transition. People are seeking work-from-home opportunities, changing careers, starting their own businesses, retiring earlier than they had planned, or choosing not to work for money at all. These changes can be exciting, and they can be terrifying. But no one has to do it alone.

This book is intended to be a guide, a support system, and a handbook for navigating these personal and professional choices. You can use the approach in this book to plan and execute your own career transitions and to manage the trajectory of your professional career, whether you are just on the cusp of starting your career or striving toward a satisfying finish. This book is a tool for life.

Using the Professional Careers by Design™ (PCD) process, you will be prepared to:

- ✓ Discern the things that matter most to you in making career decisions and use those core values to continually shape your choices.

- ✓ Manage significant career transitions, understanding where you are in the transition cycle of your career, and using that information to plan and implement the action items and strategies for navigating each stage of the Career Transitions Cycle.

- ✓ See your career in the context of your larger life and understand that your own career context is shaped by developmental tasks and core strategies that help you to move intentionally through the life course of your career.

There are three core components of the Professional Careers by Design™ model, described in this figure.

The Professional Careers by Design™ Model

Discernment	Managing Change	Lifelong Context
What Matters Most to You?	*The Career Transitions Cycle*	*The Life Course of a Career*

Figure 2: Professional Careers by Design™ Model

I use this framework to organize the book and related tools, tips, strategies, and case studies. Using this approach, the Professional Careers by Design™ process will offer specific tools and tips to help you:

✓ Understand the key career questions you are facing right now

✓ Use a straightforward, five-step process to define what matters most to you (your core values) and answer your key career questions

✓ List the Very Next Actions you need to take to implement your decision

✓ Identify how you got where you are in your career

✓ Determine when—and how—to make your next career move

✓ Understand the natural flow of your career over the course of your entire life

✓ Make a long-term Capstone Plan to see you through a career that brings you more of what matters most to you

So come along with me on this journey as I share my approach to Professional Careers by Design™.

1

What is a Designed Career?

The Professional Careers by Design™ Model

L et's begin with a short explanation of what this process is, and how my understanding of it developed. Here's my definition of Professional Careers by Design™:

Professional Careers by Design™ *is a process of knowing yourself, your current environment, and the opportunities around you in a way that lets you make informed and thoughtful decisions about your career in any given moment, no matter the circumstances or choices before you.*

That definition of this process evolved out of my work with clients and colleagues over the years. People have been using this approach on their careers successfully for over a dozen years.

So why did I write a book about career planning using this method? Career advice is all around us. Comments such as, "Do what you love and you'll never work a day in your life," or "I have to create my own luck," or "I have to put in my time before I can move up" are a dime a dozen. However, the world has changed a lot in the past few years, and a lot of our old ideas about work don't work very well anymore. It may finally be time to retire the old adages and shift to something that works better for more of us—no matter what is happening in the world around us.

This book is written for the person who has skills and dreams, who struggles to align the professional aspects of life with what matters most to them personally, and who wants a clear and reliable approach to making career decisions when possibilities arise. He may be looking at a tremendous career opportunity but concerned his caregiving obligations may mean missing out on "the chance of a lifetime." Or, she may have just been downsized by her company and seeking a stable source of income before tackling longer-term career goals, like spending more time on work that has meaning and purpose. In another case, he may have just been promoted to a new leadership role but feels concerned about the implications for his life as a single parent—he wants to succeed at both. Whatever the situation, having a compass and the skills to navigate uncertainty can help keep you on a professional path that works best for your career—and the rest of your life.

The Professional Careers by Design™ (PCD) process will help, even if you are not currently looking for a new job but are seeking a way to improve your career options within your organization, to decide whether to accept a major project, or to enhance your visibility or skill set in your current role. This process is designed for any stage of professional life.

An Important Note:

For the purposes of this book, I choose to take a broad view of what is considered a profession. The Merriam-Webster dictionary defines a profession as "a calling requiring specialized knowledge and often long and intensive academic preparation," and "a principal calling, vocation or employment."[2] Others have said that professions have key characteristics, including

---

[2] "Profession." Merriam-Webster.Com Dictionary 2022. Accessed August 15, 2022. https://www.merriam-webster.com/dictionary/profession.

accountability, responsibility for work of high importance, development of specialized knowledge, institutional preparation, and a responsibility to follow appropriate ethical constraints.[3] I agree with those definitions, but intend for this book to be inclusive of people who work in many endeavors, including the arts and creative fields, technology, and innovative new fields that may not have a formal training program, as well as those in careers more traditionally considered to be professions.

In short, this book is written for YOU, wherever you may be in your life and career, however you define your career, and whatever career decisions you are facing. For some of you, the idea of career design may sound complicated, but it really isn't. The process requires that you do a series of self-reflections at the outset. Then, you simply repeat key elements of that self-reflection on a regular basis, including any time there is a major shift in your life.

This book will describe the process in detail, but first let's put things in context with a review of some common career planning concepts.

Not Your Mother's Ten-Year Career Plan

When I think back to the way I was taught to think about my career, the common approach included mapping out my one-year, three-year, five-year, and ten-year career plans. It turns out that forty years ago, that process mostly worked. Fast-forward to today, though, and we need a new model. As the pace of information sharing, opportunities, and innovation have sped up, the pace of job changes and career decisions has accelerated dramatically. I've discovered from my work as an executive coach that for many of us, it's hard to see more than three to six months around the

---

[3] On Thu, Christian. "Fundamental Characteristics of a Profession." AALEP. Association of Accredited Public Policy Advocates to the European Union, March 10, 2016. http://www.aalep.eu/fundamental-characteristics-profession.

corner. That's why I developed the approach outlined in this book, one that has served me and many clients well.

A long-term career plan can serve as an aspirational guide, but it turns out that it needs flexibility. The day I first fully understood that need was the morning of 9/11/2001. Many of us over a certain age know exactly where we were that day, when hijacked planes hit their targets throughout the northeastern United States, and I'm no exception. I was living and working in the Midwest of the United States and found myself driving a colleague to the medical school office where I worked. This colleague was scheduled to give a presentation to our freshman students that morning. We had just arrived on campus after a breakfast meeting when my assistant met us in the parking lot and told us the news. My colleague lived in Washington, DC, near the Pentagon. As he learned what happened, he became understandably laser-focused on how to get home to his wife and his newborn baby. Everything we had planned for that morning was upended. We managed to secure what was probably the last rental car available in our area for him, and he set out on a long drive home.

Meanwhile, I turned my attention to our freshman medical students, who had just started their training three weeks prior. I was dean of students for the freshman campus, and I knew those students were overwhelmed. The students I remember most clearly were the ones who needed to leave campus and return to their distant homes to support family, friends, and loved ones. Many students came in that day to talk. The conversations of that day and the days that followed crystallized and even changed career decisions. Some students even left medical school. For good. All because of the events of that one momentous day.

As years have passed since then, I have recognized that there are many seminal events that cause people to re-evaluate their life plans. The COVID-19 pandemic is our latest example. As a coach, I have had a front-row seat for the Great Resignation[4] as many people revisit the decisions that have framed their work and personal lives and begin questioning the assumptions they have made about work in the context of their lives. People are rethinking the working conditions they want, need, and are willing to tolerate. Whatever three-, five-, or ten-year plans they had in 2018 or 2019 seem a distant memory.

These are some of the reasons the career design approach I describe will **not** ask you to create such a long-term plan. Any plan you develop could be outdated before the ink is dry. Instead, I will ask you to answer what has become my signature coaching question—a question that will serve as a touchstone throughout your life. I'll preface the question with this bit of context. A dear mentor of mine, Dr. Lois Nora, has taught me this:

Personal and professional, it's all one life. We have a finite amount of life energy, and it's up to us how we spend it.[5]

My friend Lois came to this understanding after a serious personal tragedy occurred at the height of a successful career. In sharing this lesson with me, she fundamentally shaped my approach to my own career decisions, and my approach to helping my clients make their own choices. Understanding this concept that it's up to us how we spend our time and energy cuts through the idea of finding work-life balance and asks us to focus on the things that matter most.

Here is my signature coaching question, developed over many years of experimenting with the concept that Lois taught me, and which I shared above:

---

[4] Cohen, Arianne. "How to Quit Your Job in the Great Post-Pandemic Resignation Boom." *Bloomberg Business Week* (New York), May 10, 2021. https://www.bloomberg.com/news/articles/2021-05-10/quit-your-job-how-to-resign-after-covid-pandemic#xj4y7vzkg.

[5] Nora, Lois M. *Personal Conversation (Electronic Permission Granted and on File)* (Philadelphia, PA), April 20, 2009.

What matters most to you right now? Work and home, it's all one life.
How do you want to spend your time and energy in that life?

As we move forward together in this process of Professional Careers by Design™, keep that question, and your answers to it, foremost in your mind.

Core Concepts, Key Takeaways, and Very Next Actions – Notes About How to Use This Book

At the end of each chapter in this book, I summarize the Core Concepts for the chapter and ask you to write down your Key Takeaways and Very Next Actions. Allow me to explain these ideas because they are key to making this book and its processes most useful to you.

"Core Concepts" are the big ideas from a chapter, distilled into four or five bullet points that summarize what I hope you have learned. I will provide these at the end of each chapter. I will also ask you to reflect on what your "Key Takeaways" are from each chapter. This is *your* distillation of the ideas and learnings that matter most to you. Your Key Takeaways may not be the same as my list of Core Concepts—with your different lens and life experience, you may see something very different in this material than anyone else does.

Once you have reviewed my Core Concepts and distilled your Key Takeaways, ask yourself what you are going to *do* with that information. What one or two next steps do you want to take because of what you have learned? I call these your "Very Next Actions," or VNAs for short. These should be small, clear action steps you can complete in a few days that will move you forward. I use this approach at the end of my coaching sessions, and I (and my clients) can tell you it works. This process will help you synthesize the material and move toward action, making what you learn more than just an academic exercise. It helps you move forward.

Your Very Next Actions – A Deeper Dive

VNAs sound so simple, but how can they be so effective? What is it about VNAs that turns ideas into actions? This idea is distilled from a professional lifetime of studying productivity habits and the neuroscience of human work, and helping my clients implement those habits and concepts in ways that serve them.

You may have experience starting a large project or setting an audacious goal for yourself. If you have been successful doing that, you probably already understand that you must break down large or complicated goals into smaller chunks of work. You need to mark the accomplishment of those incremental tasks, or your brain gets fatigued, and you may even feel hopeless at the daunting amount of work ahead of you.

When I am working with clients on big goals or projects, I ask them to break the work down into progressively smaller segments, until they get down to the Very Next Action they need to take. The thing that, if they get it done TODAY, will move the goal or project forward in a meaningful way. It won't get the project done or the goal fully met, but it will result in noticeable progress. It's the idea of noticeable progress that our human brains care about. We get a little jolt of neurotransmitters that our brain likes every time we make noticeable progress, but it's only powerful if we make note of it.

That's the idea behind the VNAs I will be asking you to develop as we move deeper into the Professional Careers by Design™ model. When I ask you to describe your VNA for a part of this process, I'm looking for one small step that can move you toward your goals in a way that your brain can feel good about. It might be talking to your boss about advancement opportunities or starting a conversation with your significant other about your preferred places to live. It might be making a list of the things you care about. It could be outlining what you want to negotiate for in your next job. It could be anything, but it needs to be small enough so that you can ***get it***

done in a reasonable amount of time and give your brain that little reward, so you stay motivated.

Do you recall that I said that Professional Careers by Design™ is a lifelong process? Well, your brain can't stay motivated to complete a "lifelong" task. It will only stay motivated if you focus on small steps that you can recognize and celebrate, so they can register between your ears. Over time, your progress will add up—and eventually you can write your memoirs about the whole journey—but while you are on the path, it's about hiking the next mile, not the next hundred.

So, keep these ideas in mind when I ask you to create a VNA—keep it small, doable, and noticeable. And celebrate when you complete each one!

CHAPTER 1 TOOL

Purpose of the exercise

Understanding the things that matter most to you can help you prioritize areas you may want to strengthen or improve in your life. This exercise will help you to create the list of these things so that you can gain clarity about your next steps.

Instructions

Answer the following questions using your own language. Any thoughts you include are valid, and you cannot make a list that is wrong. Make a list of the TOP TEN things that MATTER MOST TO YOU. These things should include items from your work life and your personal life. Work and life – it's all one thing.

There is no right or wrong ratio of work to personal, and you do NOT have to share this list with anyone unless you choose to. Some examples might include "family time" or "living near my parents for caregiving purposes" or "opportunity for career advancement/promotion" or "adequate salary to be financially secure."

☐ _____   ☐ _____
☐ _____   ☐ _____
☐ _____   ☐ _____
☐ _____   ☐ _____
☐ _____   ☐ _____

What surprises you about this list?

How will you use this list to guide you in making personal and professional decisions?

CHAPTER 1 – SUMMARY

Core Concepts

- The evolution of work in our society has created a clear need for a flexible, easy, and effective process for making career changes. The Professional Careers by Design™ framework will help you stay grounded in the things that matter most to you as you navigate professional and personal situations.

- Professional Careers by Design™ is not the same thing as making a five- or ten-year career plan. It's dynamic and responsive to whatever surprises life may throw you.

- Career planning and strategy is a lifelong process, not a one-time choice.

- The Professional Careers by Design™ model is intended to recognize that work and personal priorities and obligations make up our one life. Our life energy is finite, and we get to choose how we spend our time and energy in both our personal and professional lives.

Key Takeaways

What are your Key Takeaways from this chapter? What did you learn, in your own words?

Very Next Actions

What Are Your Very Next Actions (VNAs) based on what you have learned in this chapter?

What are one or two small, achievable steps you want to take to get more of those things that matter most to you into your life?

VNA #1:

VNA #2:

Fundamental Life Design Concepts

Introduction to Design Thinking for Careers

'm sure you're ready to start designing the career of your dreams, but we need to walk before we can run. And it will help if we start with a common understanding of some fundamental concepts, so that you can use them to develop your understanding of career strategy, planning, and the intentionally designed career. You might find it helpful to take some notes for yourself as you go through this list. What are you learning about yourself as you explore these concepts? Which ideas are most important to you at this stage of your life and career? Your reflections will be valuable as we dive deeper into the design process for your career.

Design Thinking

The basic idea of Design Thinking arises from work done by Bill Burnett and Dave Evans from Stanford University, who wrote the book *Designing Your Life: How to Build a Well-Lived, Joyful Life*,[6] and who teach a very

---

[6] Burnett, Bill, and Dave Evans. 2016. *Designing Your Life: How to Build a Well-Lived, Joyful Life*. New York: Alfred A. Knopf. Reproduced with permission (electronic permission on file).

popular course of the same name for students there. Their core approach includes the following key attributes:

- Curiosity
- Bias to action
- Reframing
- Awareness
- Radical Collaboration

For our purposes in this book, the action steps from Design Thinking that seem most relevant to me are these:

1. Stay curious about what is going on for you.
2. Try things, even if they don't work out.
3. Reframe your beliefs about your situation.
4. Understand that your life and career require an ongoing process of decision-making.
5. Ask others for help.

Broader work on Design Thinking,[7] as described by Plattner, Meinel and Liefer, is also useful for our thinking about Professional Careers by Design™.[8] Design Thinking involves innovation based on a process of defining and redefining a problem and testing out various solutions. Solving the wicked problems that can come up in a career by thinking outside the box and looking for creative options is a way of bringing Design Thinking to career decision-making.

———————————

[7] Wikipedia. 2023. "Design Thinking." Wikimedia Foundation. Last modified May 14, 2023. https://en.wikipedia.org/wiki/Design_thinking.

[8] Plattner, Hasso, Christoph Meinel, and Larry Leifer. 2011. *Design Thinking: Understand, Improve, Apply. Understanding Innovation*. Berlin: Springer-Verlag.

What this mindset requires is that you understand you can make change, and that there really are no "failures"—only experiments about what works for you. The Professional Careers by Design™ model helps you determine which experiments you want to try, assess the risks you are willing and able to take at this stage of your life, and then own the rewards from the innovative design work you are doing. Design Thinking also asks you to be open to choices working out differently than you may have expected.

Throughout this book, I will ask you to utilize Design Thinking concepts as you build your intentionally designed career. Pay particular attention to activities that ask you to stay curious, try things, reframe your thinking, make iterative change, and ask for help. When you do those things, you are practicing Design Thinking.

Values

For our purposes, the term ***values*** refers to the things that we hold as important, useful, and meaningful to us. Values may be concepts such as ideals or character qualities, and they can also be more tangible things like time with family, money, power, fame, or opportunity. People tend to have a set of fundamental values that are instilled in them early in life by the people and culture around them. They also tend to learn and grow as individuals and develop a more personal set of values based on life experiences. In the last chapter, I asked you to complete an exercise around my signature coaching question, "What matters most to you right now?" Your answers are essentially a distillation of your values at this stage of your life.

As you might have noticed when you completed that exercise, your values at any given moment are defined by myriad factors—your upbringing, heritage, and life circumstances at the present time are some of the most influential. If you have young children, for example, you may put a premium on time with them, such as being home for dinner and bedtime, or making time for extracurricular games and performances. Your life as a parent influences your values and priorities while your children need you most. Similarly, if you have aging parents or others in your circle who require caregiving from you, your value of caring for family may shift the priorities for your career during this time. Conversely, if you are a new professional just trying to make your mark in the world, your value of career advancement may focus your priorities on gaining influence at work. Values tend to be static, but the way in which they are prioritized shifts over time, and your age and stage of life and career will influence how you prioritize competing values.

Rewards

There are many things that we may hold dear and consider to be valuable enough that they can change our behavior and choices. We sometimes think of these things as **rewards**. In the world of psychology, rewards are thought of as positive reinforcement for our behaviors. The list of things that people consider to be rewards varies, but there are some that most people agree on. These include what I think of as the primary currencies of the professional world: time, money, power, information, and prestige. But those aren't the only rewards. A nice parking space or a corner office can be a reward. A trophy or prize might be meaningful. As you think about the professional rewards you care about, it can be helpful to divide them into these categories:

- Monetary rewards
  - Compensation (salary and benefits)
  - Non-compensation (other things that have monetary value, such as payment for continuing education or professional dues)

- Non-monetary rewards
  - Flexible scheduling and remote work
  - Opportunities for advancement

- Sponsorship to enhance your influence and visibility in your field of expertise

Consider the rewards that matter to you as you think about how to make career choices. If something simply doesn't matter to you (for example, if you bike to work, that parking place holds no value for you), then, of course, it should not drive your career choices. It will take something different to motivate you. Also consider that just like values, the rewards and incentives that matter to you may change over time. If you are a caregiver, you may feel that your time (for caregiving or self-care) is more important to you than money. If that's the case, an additional two weeks of paid time off may be a far greater reward than a raise.

It's important to understand the rewards that drive your current decision-making.

Stakeholders

Your decisions about your career will affect you most of all, but you won't be the only person affected—not remotely.

Whenever I start working with a client who is considering a career transition, I ask them to list their *stakeholders*. When folks struggle to make this list, I ask them, "Who would care most if your next career decision meant that you moved to another country or were away from home for an extended period of time?" Those are your core *personal stakeholders*. Your core *professional stakeholders* are the people whose own work responsibilities and roles would be meaningfully affected by your career decisions.

People's lists of stakeholders vary, but they commonly include members of their nuclear family: spouse or partner, children, sometimes parents, or even pets, for example. Stakeholder lists may also include a boss, colleagues, and employees.

It's your career. Why all this focus on others? I ask people to list their stakeholders, so they can decide if those stakeholders hold enough sway to influence the career decision at hand. Not all stakeholders should get a say in your next decision, though some might. Some stakeholders might not want to sway your decision anyway, though their respect for your decision-making process means they will support your choices.

Regardless, you get to decide which stakeholders have a say, and to do this, you must first identify them as stakeholders. You may want to consult some of them as we go along in this process.

Our Changing View of Work

Remember when I saw my students' worldview shift at work? It was the morning of 9/11. For many other people, their seminal moment came during the COVID-19 pandemic, but moments like this don't have to be global. They can also be local, like a personal tragedy. The effect is the same: life changes. And so, *our view of work and the workplace changes over time*. Circumstances shift, and decisions that were very much aligned with our personal and professional needs a few years ago may no longer serve us or our stakeholders well. When we understand that life brings cycles of change—and that it's no failure to change your mind and head off in another career direction—the idea of designing your career gets easier and may even become an exciting adventure.

You may be someone who thought you would have one career, even one job, for your whole life. That was true for many of our parents. But that kind of job and the reciprocal corporate loyalty to employees it requires have become scarce. Changing business models and mindsets have shown many of today's professionals that downsizing, offshoring, and other trends mean they must be more nimble, moving around the workplace to build skills, enhance their network, and maximize their own opportunities. Meanwhile, many people are working into their seventies and beyond, and the shifting job market requires flexibility, emotional intelligence, and an ability to navigate rapid and frequent change.

Curveballs Will Happen to You!

Even if the changing nature of the workplace hasn't really affected you, you shouldn't assume it won't. In addition, there is a corollary concept that we should talk about here. If you're experiencing a period of wild success, it's easy to become complacent. You may feel you are at the top of your game and that you have achieved your dream job. Why even worry about what's next? But change does happen, and *it likely will happen to you.*

Sometimes the need for change sneaks up on us, like a curveball in baseball. Curveballs can be positive opportunities (someone calls you from a recruiting firm and asks you to apply for a seemingly wonderful job in a city in which you'd love to live) or negative challenges (your company furloughs you due to budget cuts, or your spouse develops a serious medical condition that changes your lives dramatically).

This process of crafting a Professional Career by Design™ will require that you think ahead about curveballs, both good and bad. The act of considering these possibilities before they happen can help you be ready when life inevitably happens.

Being the CEO of Your Own Career

Many of my clients start their career journeys thinking that they don't have a lot of choices—they have entered a profession, and while it may not be what they imagined, they cannot see a way to change anything. Or they believe success comes from stumbling through a series of opportunities and landing in the right place at the right time. These folks are often not *dis*-satisfied with their work, but they are not fully *satisfied* either. When I hear these themes from clients, I invite them to consider their career as an enterprise, company, business, or project that they oversee. In effect, they are the CEO of "Themselves, Inc." It's a novel concept, and one that people often struggle to adopt. That's because professional training is based on learning a set of rules about behavior, prescribed and expected by those in the profession. This is a necessary part of learning a role and understanding a type of work. But when life happens, it becomes clear that those rules don't always serve all of us all the time. Sometimes you must question the basic assumptions you may have made about your job and work life, and when you do, you start to see that you have choices. And seeing that you have choices, even if the choices aren't perfect, you can more easily find a sense of empowerment and agency that lets you move forward. That's the start of being the CEO of your career.

If this is a new concept to you, ask yourself, "How would I think about my career if I were running it as a business? Why would it be in business, and what would I want that business to do, produce, or accomplish?" This way of thinking can flip even the direst of situations upside down and help you see a way through challenges. And it can help you weigh opportunities as well.

Understanding that your career is worthy of this kind of attention is a big deal. The idea that *you* get to make the decisions that impact your career and your life based on what matters to you is at the heart of this concept, and indeed of this book.

Building a Career Board of Advisors

Now that you have named yourself CEO of You, Inc., it's time to build your Career Board of Advisors. These are the people who will provide advice and guidance while helping you see opportunities and pitfalls in your choices. They should also recognize that you are the one making the decisions. You may want to include mentors, peers, friends, or family as part of your board. Sometimes a stakeholder from our earlier discussion sits on your Board of Advisors, but the role is different. Stakeholders have a vested interest in the decisions you make, and their needs may influence your choices. Your Board of Advisors is situated to advise you in your decision-making. People who have both roles may hold both types of influence, and you may need to clarify for them whether you want their advice or are taking their needs into consideration. In this situation, it is important that you have clarity and can communicate it to them as well.

Key advisors typically fall into one of several categories. You may want to include all these categories, or only some of them.

- Professional advisors
  - Legal advisors
  - Financial advisors (accountant, financial planner)
- Profession-based advisors
  - People *in your field* who are senior to you and who may have already helped you make career decisions. These are typically discipline-based experts who are ahead of you on the same or a similar career path to you.
  - Peers *in your field* who are at the same stage of life/career that you are, whose counsel you value, and for whom you likely provide insight and input as well.
- Spiritual advisors. This can be someone who has a formal role in your life, such as a minister, or someone who simply shares a similar worldview and outlook as you.
- Personal advisors. Often a spouse or partner falls into this category because he may have significant input and influence on your decision-making. But it could also be a sibling, close friend, or someone else with whom your connection is primarily personal. Don't forget about the need for clarity with her about whether you want her advice or are taking her personal needs into consideration in your decision-making.

These people are all potential candidates for your Board of Advisors. Some of them (if you are lucky) will have permanent seats on your Board, staying with you throughout your lifetime and seeing the story of your career develop. Others will serve a role for a time, then will rotate off your Board. That's OK. Not all seats are permanent. For this Board, you get to decide. This approach to selecting a team of guides is intended to help you think about the kind of input and wisdom you might need, so you can select the right people. It is unlikely any one person will have all the expertise you need, and it's very freeing to realize you don't have to find the perfect mentor. While mentors, sponsors (who bring you opportunities to advance your influence or visibility while mentoring you), and family all have a role to play, shaping a career is definitely not a one-person job.

Additional Thoughts on Design Thinking for Careers

Bringing a Design Thinking approach to your career decisions is another way of challenging your assumptions about work and the trajectory of your work life. Its iterative mindset is a lens for staying fluid and flexible as our world of work (and our personal circumstances) ebb and flow. Finally, it suggests that you seek counsel from multiple "wise others." In short, it is the lens we need to adapt to our modern world of work. You are the CEO, you have this Board of Advisors, and you know what matters most to you. You get to decide what opportunities to pursue, which ones to let pass, and what chances and risks you want to take. When you embrace Design Thinking, you gain a perspective that can lead to outcomes you never dreamed of, and a level of satisfaction and alignment in your work and personal life that will amaze you.

It is this kind of thinking that led to the development of the Professional Careers by Design™ approach. It is also this kind of thinking that my coaching clients have used to build meaningful and successful careers.

Intentionally Designed Careers – a Brief Recap

An intentionally designed career asks an individual to continually reflect on the things that matter most to her—to iteratively assess those things against the needs of her stakeholders, the context of her work life and personal life, and the circumstances in the larger world around her. And then to use that information to make the very best decision available to her in the moment. A career designer is not afraid to try new things. She balances risk with the knowledge that she has choices, and she gets to make the decisions. If something doesn't work out, she can begin the process again. A career designer is comfortable asking herself tough questions, curious about her own life, and fearless enough to prototype a new approach. And her career will be custom-designed for her—and her priorities. At every stage of her life and career.

CHAPTER 2 TOOL

Purpose of the exercise

These questions are intended to help you think creatively and proactively about your career. Use them as guideposts for developing a design thinking approach to your career.

Instructions

Use the What Matters Most to You worksheet from the last chapter to help you craft your answers to these design questions for your career.

- What are the core values that drive you?

- What are the rewards that may be important to you at this point in your career journey?

- Who are your stakeholders, and how do you want them to be involved in your career decision-making process?

- What do you know about the ways you view work and the workplace? How have your views changed over time?

- How could curveballs show up in your life, both as opportunities and as challenges?

- How might you approach your career differently if you thought of that career as a business enterprise, and of yourself as the CEO of that business?

- Who is already on your Career Board of Advisors, and who might you need to add, replace or remove?

- How will you use your answers to these questions in order to guide you in making personal and professional decisions?

CHAPTER 2 – SUMMARY

Core Concepts

- The principles of Design Thinking—including curiosity, an iterative mindset, a willingness to seek input from wise others and open-mindedness when choices work out differently than you expect—will support and enhance your journey through lifelong career decision-making.

- You have core values that drive your work and life priorities and decisions, rewards that matter to you as you make those choices, and a set of stakeholders whom your decisions will affect. Understanding how those concepts show up in your life is a necessary part of the self-reflection process that enables great career choices.

- How you view work will change over your lifetime, and you will continually find yourself questioning the assumptions you make about your work life and workplace. Personal, local, and global circumstances will influence these assumptions.

- Career design is dynamic. Reflecting on your assumptions about work any time something shifts in your life will keep your decisions aligned with your priorities. The process of assessing the degree of alignment between your personal and professional life changes with the circumstances and seasons of your life. The model of Professional Careers by Design™ is built on the assumption that this assessment process is ongoing throughout your lifetime.

- You are in charge of your career. Understanding that you have choices enables you to act in your own interest and that of your key stakeholders. Be the CEO of your own career and establish a Board of Advisors to support you along the way.

Key Takeaways

What are your Key Takeaways from this chapter? What did you learn, in your own words?

Very Next Actions

What Are Your Very Next Actions (VNAs) based on what you have learned in this chapter?

How will your values and personal reward structure shape your career choices? What actions do you need to take now that you know more about these ideas?

VNA #1:

VNA #2:

PART 2

Discernment – What Matters Most to You?

S o, what exactly is this career design process I keep talking about? In this part of the book, we will determine the key questions you are (or think you should be) asking about your career. Then we will dive into the Five Key Steps of Discernment—which are shared as a set of Hip Pocket Questions, a reusable set of queries that you can keep in your mind, in your wallet, or some other handy place and that encourage you to update your career design process anytime a change or decision is called for.

Remember my definition of this overall process:

Professional Careers by Design™ *is a process of knowing yourself, your current environment, and the opportunities around you in a way that lets you make informed and thoughtful decisions about your career in any given moment, no matter the circumstances or choices before you.*

The three pillars of the process are:

1. Discernment of what matters most to you

2. Management of career change

3. Understanding the lifelong context of your career

This section of the book focuses on that first pillar, discernment of what matters most to you. Here, I will share with you an approach to finding your own answers to this question, and a way to consider the wants and needs of others who are important to you as well. We will begin by focusing on the career questions you are dealing with right now, in this season of your life, so you can gain clarity about what you are questioning and what you need to figure out about your career, your larger life beyond work, and how those things fit together.

In this section, I will share tools and tips, as well as case studies based on real people. I have crafted their stories as composites from many different coaching clients with whom I have worked. No single story represents any real individual, and please treat them as composite stories designed for the purpose of illustrating key concepts while protecting individuals' identity.

Let's jump in!

What Career Questions Are You Asking Yourself?

A Bit of Context

Each of us comes to our careers with a set of hopes and dreams for where we will land. We don't always know how things will work out, but we often have a general sense. When I start working with clients, I find that they generally bring one of two approaches to career planning to our work. The first involves "climbing the ladder," checking off boxes as they go, and moving "up," though it's not always clear to them what "up" looks like. Sometimes they wonder whether their ladder is leaning against the right wall. These individuals often find themselves frustrated as they advance because the view from the middle of the ladder, or even from the top rung, is not what they expected. I often meet these people at mid-career when they seek coaching either because they:

- realize they've become disillusioned
- feel ready to build their own ladder and redefine what it means to climb

The second approach I commonly see is what Mary Catherine Bateson describes as discontinuity in her book, *Composing a Life.*[9] People who take this approach tell me, "I just got lucky. I was in the right place at the right time, and never really planned my career formally." They are sometimes satisfied with where they end up, but they may be wondering why they have not been selected for advancement or new positions. They may have a highly refined set of relationships that they know how to leverage (this may in fact be the origin of their perceived "luck"). They may not really understand the politics of their profession, organization, or team and feel stuck as a result. Clients often call this approach "the flight of the bumblebee." When I meet people who have taken this approach, it's often either because they:

- feel their luck has run out, and they can't figure out how to get back on track.

- are being recruited for an advanced position they can't imagine they are ready or qualified to accept.

No one approach to career design is right or wrong, but I have seen hundreds of people become unstuck when they embrace a more strategic approach that borrows from each of these approaches and grounds them in core values and priorities.

Professional Careers by Design™ is not just for those who are mid-career, senior in their field, getting promoted beyond their confidence level, or hitting a wall. This model is for everyone, and the earlier in your career that you adopt the Professional Careers by Design™ approach, the more intentional your decisions will be—and the more successful you will be, no matter what circumstances life presents. The sooner you start, the more alignment you will find between what you are doing to make a living

---

[9] Bateson, Mary C. 2001. *Composing a Life.* New York: Grove Press.

and what you are doing to make a life for yourself and those you care about. This is truly a Bespoke Life.

Way Markers on the Road to Transition

The first step in this process of designing your career is to get clear on the questions you are facing. Are you getting started in a new job and trying to set yourself up for success? Are you doing fine in your job but a little bored and wondering where you might go next? Is your organization downsizing, leaving you afraid you may lose your job? Has someone reached out to recruit you for a great new opportunity? Do you have a new family member like a spouse or child, or a family member who is ill, causing you to think about how to manage your work life amid new personal challenges?

These are common questions that compel people to take a second look at their career choices, but they are certainly not the only questions to consider. The questions of the moment for each individual also link to the stage of career and career transition in which they find themselves at any given moment. More on this in Parts 3 and 4 of this book.

The Career Circumstances Quiz

We are going to do a deep dive into these concepts later in the book, but for now, I've created a short quiz to help you clarify where you are in the career transition process and to help you focus on the current career questions you are facing. Use the tool that follows here to consider and write down those questions.

CHAPTER 3 TOOL

Purpose of the exercise

This quiz will help you determine where in the Career Change Cycle you currently find yourself, and will help you develop the two or three Key Career Questions that are most important to you right now.

Instructions

Review the brief scenarios below. Think about where you are in your own career journey right now, and choose the ONE scenario that is CLOSEST to describing your own stage on that journey at the present time. Then take a few minutes to write down for yourself the most important Key Career Questions you are facing at this stage of your journey.

A. I am in a job that makes me happy and satisfied. I'm not considering any changes to my career at all.

B. Something has happened (good or bad) that has made me start thinking about a career change.

C. I am actively searching for a new opportunity. I've submitted applications or letters of interest, or I'm interviewing for new positions.

D. I am negotiating for one or more new positions. I've received at least one offer and am negotiating terms for those positions while still in my current job.

E. I'm in an active transition between jobs. I have a new position I'm headed for and am trying to wrap up my current role.

F. I am in a new job and trying to figure out how to be successful.

Which lettered scenario best describes your current circumstances: _ _ _ _ _ _ _ _ _ _

Key Career Question #1:

Key Career Question #2:

Key Career Question #3:

CHAPTER 3 – SUMMARY

Core Concepts

- Many people believe their professional success involves climbing a ladder to accomplishment, while others describe their success as a result of luck. Professional Careers by Design™ borrows from these and other models, and what sets it apart is the way it integrates your values and priorities with your career stage, current job circumstances and lifelong context.

- The first step in the Discernment portion of the Professional Careers by Design™ process is to frame the key career questions you are asking yourself. It helps to have a sense of the context for your current career circumstances. That context will help you understand the key questions you are facing in the moment.

- Framing your key career questions will help you be ready to consider the next step in the discernment process, as it relates to the most relevant issues you are facing right now.

Key Takeaways

What are your Key Takeaways from this chapter? What did you learn, in your own words?

Very Next Actions

What Are Your Very Next Actions (VNAs) based on what you have learned in this chapter?

Look at your answers to the Key Career Questions that you wrote down in the exercise above. How might you start gathering answers to your key career questions?

VNA #1:

VNA #2:

4

Deeper Discernment – Asking Important Questions of Yourself and Others

The Steps of Deeper Discernment

Now that you have a sense of the questions you are asking yourself, it's time to go deeper in figuring out what is important to you. I teach people a five-step approach to deepening their understanding of the career issues they are facing. Each step includes a key question you must be able to answer in the context of the current circumstances in your personal and professional life. The steps and their associated questions are:

1. Knowing Yourself: What matters most to you personally and professionally at this age and stage of your life?

2. Knowing Your Stakeholders: Who are the people in your life with a stake in the decisions you make, and what matters most to them?

3. Knowing Your Environment: What matters most to your current employer (even if that employer is you)?

4. Assessing the Alignment: Are there any misalignments among the answers in Steps 1, 2 and 3?

5. Making a Decision: If there are misalignments, what are you ready and able to do about them right now? If there are no misalignments, how do you want to grow?

We are going to explore each of those steps in more detail in the coming sections. The first three steps of this process rely on your own curiosity about what drives you, what and who matter to you, and what matters to the organization or entity in which your professional life is situated. Curiosity, you may remember, is a core part of the Design Thinking approach to careers. Curiosity helps us to stay open, gain insight about our own motivations, and use that information to define the question at hand.

The last two steps are really about that Design Thinking concept of prototyping. What is the problem you are trying to solve, and what solution can you put forward, knowing that you can always try a different solution if needed? Keep these ideas in mind—approaching the process from a stance of curiosity, defining the question you face clearly, and making the very best career decision you can make with the information available to you, then repeating the process whenever it's needed.

Step 1: Knowing Yourself

The core question for this step is that favorite question of mine, "What matters most to you, personally and professionally, at this age and stage of your life?" The answers to this question change with circumstance. Revisit the worksheet you completed at the end of Chapter 1 and be curious about the list you made. What did you learn about your top priorities? Did they surprise you?

Think again about what your core values are, and the rewards that matter to you. Maybe salary or money is at the top of your list, and maybe not. Perhaps time with your family while your children are still at home is the most important thing. Perhaps cementing your professional reputation and making a definitive niche in your profession for yourself is most important. No judgments—it's your list, and you can't be wrong. Whatever the important things are, you must identify them because they are the foundation for this whole process.

The key question for Step 1 of the deeper discernment process is, "What matters most to you personally and professionally, right now?"

Step 2: Knowing Your Stakeholders

Who are the people in your life with a stake in the decisions you make, and what matters most to them? When I am working with a client, I ask them this question: If you decided to make your next career move halfway around the world, where another language is primary and the living conditions are much different, who would care? Who would be affected by that decision? And what would they have to say about it? The answers to these questions will help you zero in on who your stakeholders are and the ways they could influence (or not influence) your career decisions.

Start by making a list of your key stakeholders. For most people, this list includes a spouse or significant other, children, and perhaps parents or grandparents. It might include your colleagues or your boss, but they do not have to be on the list. For what it's worth, some people even include their pets as key stakeholders. Think about taking your cat with you to a new job in Asia—that would take some planning!

Why do I ask you to take the time to make this list? Because your stakeholders are people who will affect and be affected by whatever you decide. When you clarify their stake in your decision, you are better able to see how their wants, needs, and goals might shape your decisions. When it's right, you can allow them to influence the choices you make.

Once you have made your list, revisit the question from our first step, but with a twist. What matters most to THEM? If they are of an age to be able to tell you, you can ask them. You might even share that worksheet from Chapter 1 with them and ask them to make their own Top Ten List of What Matters Most. If you do that, don't make your lists together. Do them separately and then compare notes.

Identifying your stakeholders, deciding whether each one should have a stake in your decision, and then either inquiring or projecting what you think matters to them are all part of your stakeholder analysis. Not only will this process help you consider your decision in the context of the people you care about but it may also clarify your own list of what matters to you. One of your priorities may move up your list because of its importance to one or more of your stakeholders.

The key question for Step 2 of the deeper discernment process is "Who are your key stakeholders and what matters most to them?"

Step 3: Knowing Your Environment

Once you have a good idea of what matters most to you and to your key stakeholders, it is time to turn your attention to your employer. What matters most to that organization? Is it the bottom line of money? Are there particularly important shareholders in the company or stakeholders for the organization? Is the key outcome reputation? Market share? Being seen as an industry leader? Are there considerations about political power or other issues that seem to drive priorities and the use of resources?

Whatever the priorities of your organization, it is imperative that you understand them. I'll explain why in Step 4. For now, consider how you might learn about the priorities of the organization. You may hear them clearly articulated in regular meetings or in messages from the leadership. There may be a mission, vision, or values statement intended to serve as a touchstone for setting priorities. Organizations adhere to such statements with varying degrees of fidelity, but if those documents are available, it is important to consider them. Strategic planning documents and processes may also yield clues.

It is important to recognize that leaders bring their own interpretation to organizational priorities, mission, vision, and values, and each leadership team will have varying degrees of success in achieving their goals. Sometimes you have to get to know the leadership team, listen to what they say—as well as what they do not say—and watch their actions to really gain a sense of what matters to them. You may have to talk to mentors, colleagues, or the leaders themselves. Even if you don't get face time to ask the top brass about what they want, you can piece information together to make a reasonable estimate.

If you are not employed at the moment, you may be wondering how this step applies to you. It does, though you will need to reframe these ideas and gather the same information about the potential employers you are considering. It's a useful exercise to get a sense of the landscape, regardless of your current circumstances.

The key question for Step 3 of the deeper discernment process is, "What does my organization and its leadership prioritize, and what are their stated and the unstated goals?"

Step 4: Assessing Alignment

Once you have made your way through the questions in Steps 1-3, it's time to pull together the information you've gathered. The secret to making the best decision for you and your career in the context of this information is to examine the alignment among the answers to the first three questions. You'll want to look at what is aligned and what might be misaligned as well. Often it is the simple act of identifying serious misalignments that leads people to decide to change their career trajectory. This step is the heart of the process and requires that you synthesize everything you have learned in the previous steps.

The key question for Step 4 of the deeper discernment process is, "What is the alignment between my answers to the first three questions in this process?"

Step 5: Making a Decision

Making a career decision is not as easy as it sounds. You began by determining the key career questions you are facing in the moment (see the exercise in Chapter 3). Using the first four steps of deeper discernment, you have now clarified what matters to you, the stakeholders in your life and your employer, and have identified any misalignments among all those priorities.

If you discover that there are no misalignments—fantastic! Your focus can be on determining how you will continue to learn and grow in a place and situation where you are thriving. This is really a matter of staying right where you are and growing toward more of those things that matter to you and your key stakeholders.

If, however, you find that there are misalignments, it's time to ask yourself what you are ready, willing, and able to do about those misalignments. Your choices come down to three options:

1. Stay where you are and wait it out until you *can* do something differently or change your situation.

2. Leave for a situation that is better aligned with what matters to you and your key stakeholders

3. Leave no matter what. What I mean here is, if things are truly toxic, you may not be able to wait until you have found a situation with better alignment. This may be a decision to support your own well-being or that of your key stakeholders, or it may be a decision made from necessity, such as needing to replace lost income after a downsizing, for example.

The key questions for Step 5 are either: "How do you want to learn and grow from a place where you are currently thriving and there are no misalignments?" OR "What are you ready, willing, and able to do about any misalignments you have identified?"

Repeat and Update as Needed

Remember that designing your career is a lifelong commitment, and the deeper discernment process is not just a one-time exercise for times of curiosity or crisis. I suggest to my clients that they repeat this process at least annually, perhaps on their birthday, at the start of a new year, or at some other annual milestone date that makes sense to them. I call this the "Annual Career Design Review." I also suggest that clients review their answers at least quarterly to remind themselves of where they are and whether anything has changed. Finally, if they experience a major life change, it's a good idea (after coming up for air!) to take a couple hours and work through the discernment process again to see if anything needs realignment in the face of change. In short, my clients use the process as often as they need, including at any time that things seem to be shifting. You can do the same.

The Hip Pocket Questions

The five steps we have discussed, and the key questions associated with each, are really the core of the discernment pillar of the Professional Careers by Design™ process. They are so important—and so useful—that I urge people to keep them at their fingertips. That's why I have compiled them at the end of this chapter as a worksheet for you, all in one place. It's also why I call them the Hip Pocket Questions. The idea is to ensure you can (literally or figuratively) keep this list in your hip pocket to access and review as often as you need to. The Hip Pocket Questions are the core of your discernment strategy. Use them well and share them with anyone you think will benefit.

CASE STUDY – Dylan:

Dylan is a high school English teacher who has been in his current job for ten years. His wife works locally as an events manager in the entertainment industry in a position that does not require travel. They have two children, ages seven and eleven, who are becoming more active in school and extra-curricular activities. His superintendent has offered him a promotion to a leadership role overseeing design of a new curriculum approach that will take additional time beyond his normal teaching roles.

Questions for the Reader:

1. What do you imagine the key career decision Dylan is facing might be?

2. What do you imagine Dylan's answers to the Hip Pocket Questions would be?

Dylan Speaks: I used the Hip Pocket Questions and the What Matters Most to Me exercise to determine that time with my children, as their activity level is increasing, was of prime importance. My wife and I share taxi-driver responsibilities for the kids, so it's not that I'm the only one who can do that. By using this process, I found that it really mattered to me that I be present for their activities, so I don't miss out on the experience and I can support them. I also realized that I don't want to work a lot of extra hours beyond my normal teaching duties because I like to hike and maintain an exercise routine. I truly enjoy spending time with my wife, and I just want a life outside of work. We are also fortunate enough not to have to depend on the small amount of extra money that this position would have offered.

Dylan's Outcome: Dylan turned down the promotion, and he and his wife developed a routine of attending their children's activities together whenever possible. Each of them became a coach or advisor to one of their children's extracurricular activities, and as a family, they planned weekly hikes and regular local mini-vacations throughout their children's school years.

CHAPTER 4 TOOL

Purpose of the exercise

The answers to these questions will provide a touchstone you can use to answer any career question you are facing.

Instructions

Use the tools from the earlier sections to help answer these questions. When you have answered them, keep the list where you can find it. Update the answers to these questions at least once a year, and anytime your career or personal circumstances undergo a significant change.

- **Hip Pocket Question # 1: What matters most to you, personally and professionally, right now, at this stage of your life and career?**

- **Hip Pocket Question # 2: Who are your key stakeholders, and what matters most to them?**

- **Hip Pocket Question # 3: What are your organization's priorities?**
  - **What does your organization and its leadership value most?**
  - **What are their stated goals?**
  - **What are their unstated goals?**

- **Hip Pocket Question # 4: What is the alignment (or misalignment) among your answers to the first three questions in this process?**

- **Hip Pocket Question # 5 is one of two possible questions, depending on your response at Step 4:**
  - **How do you want to learn and grow from a place where you are currently thriving and there are no misalignments?**

    OR

  - **What are you ready, willing, and able to do about any misalignments you have identified?**

CHAPTER 4 – SUMMARY

Core Concepts

- The Deeper Discernment component of the Professional Careers by Design™ model is built around a five-step process that can be repeated as often as needed. The earlier in your career you start using this process, the more intentionally designed your career will be.

- Each step in the process is linked to your answer to a key question.

- These five key questions are the Hip Pocket Questions. You should always have the answers to the Hip Pocket Questions, well, in your hip pocket.

- Update your responses to the Hip Pocket Questions at least annually, and any time your life circumstances or external circumstances change.

- Review your answers to the Hip Pocket Questions at least quarterly, and any time you are uncertain about your career path.

Key Takeaways

What are your Key Takeaways from this chapter? What did you learn, in your own words?

Very Next Actions

What Are Your Very Next Actions (VNAs) based on what you have learned in this chapter?

How will you begin the Five Steps? Which of the Hip Pocket Questions will you answer first?

VNA #1:

VNA #2:

5

Managing Curveballs

Curveballs aren't just for baseball, you know.

Even though I promised you I would not ask you to create a three-, five-, or even ten-year career plan, many clients come to me asking if they should put one together. When I hear this question from clients, I smile to myself and think, "I can't see more than two or three months around the corner, and even that is dicey these days."

In case you haven't figured it out by now, I'm not a fan of long-term career plans. We really can't predict what life will throw at us today or tomorrow, never mind next week or next year. That's why my Professional Careers by Design™ model is designed to be flexible and provide you with the tools you need to adapt thoughtfully and make decisions systematically, no matter what life throws your way.

If that's my goal—a resilient process that you can use no matter what—then we really must talk about curveballs. A curveball is generally thought to be a baseball pitch thrown with a spin to make it veer downward and to the side. Why would a pitcher want to throw such a pitch? Well, it keeps the batter on her toes, and it makes the pitch harder to hit. The batter doesn't know which way the ball is going to go and has little time to adapt once the direction of the "curve" becomes apparent. Curveballs make it a lot harder to achieve a hit.

Life is like that, though I'm not sure life's curveballs are intended to lead us astray. It's just the way life is built. How we adapt to the curves, and how quickly, can determine our success and happiness along the way. In this chapter, we will explore what Career Curveballs look like and how we can anticipate and respond to them in real time. Let's get started.

Positive curveballs

What would you do if someone came to you and offered you your dream job in a dream location, but you had to decide in one week, and be ready to start in one month? How would you make that decision? How would you know it was your dream job? How would you weigh your own dream against those of the key stakeholders in your life? How would you know if you could make it happen?

That is exactly why the Professional Careers by Design™ model was built. If you know the answers to the five Hip Pocket Questions, you have a pretty good idea of what your dream job looks like and how it fits into your personal life. You may even know where your dream job should be located and the effect it would have on key stakeholders. But could you make the decision quickly?

CASE STUDY – Amber

Amber is a faculty member at a major university who has recently been promoted to associate professor with tenure. Her job is not perfect, but she is reasonably satisfied with her work and is starting several new projects that she is interested in and motivated to pursue. Her university offers sabbaticals at various points in a faculty member's career, and she is currently eligible for such a sabbatical. Regular recruitment opportunities cross her inbox. She typically does not look closely at them, but this week, one caught her eye. She is being invited to do a one-year visiting professorship in Scotland, teaching and pursuing her existing projects while developing collaborations for future work. Amber has always dreamed of living in Scotland (she is an avid golfer). Her spouse is happily employed and has some professional commitments that cannot be left behind for at least six months but would love to travel in Europe. They have no children but have a four-year-old dog. They own a home and love it and consider it to be their retirement home.

Questions for the Reader:

1. What do you imagine the key career decision Amber is facing might be?

2. How would you suggest she go about making this decision?

Amber Speaks: Wow, what an opportunity! I didn't see this one coming. I guess the real question is, should I apply for this job, since they are actively seeking me? We would both love to spend time in Europe, but I don't know how to work out all the details. I guess I need to talk with my husband about what matters to him, and I need to think about what it would mean for me to be away from my home university for a full year. We might have to live separately until my husband could wrap up some projects, and I don't know what to do about our dog or our house. I am working on making a list of the questions I need to answer before I can decide. I'm excited, but worried about all the details.

Amber's Outcome: After significant discussion with her husband, Amber decided to take the opportunity in Scotland. Her husband wrapped up some of his projects, traveled to Scotland to see her for a week every two months until he could join her there after seven months with their dog (he managed the process of getting the dog ready to make the trip). They spent the last five months in Scotland together with their dog, with her working and them all traveling across Europe, hiking and playing golf as their time permitted. Her husband was able to develop new clients in Europe for his company. They returned to their permanent home after her visiting professorship, and she gained new collaborators, her husband got a promotion, and they both made new friends and memories they will treasure.

This scenario is an example of a "positive" curveball. It's generally a good thing, though the stress you'll face when it happens may not feel so great in the moment. Other examples of positive curveballs can be getting married, having a child, or getting a windfall inheritance that significantly changes your dependence on your salary for financial security. How can you plan for scenarios like this? Here are my key tips to prepare for the day that opportunity knocks on your door:

1. Keep your Hip Pocket Question responses up to date.

2. Make a list of all the POSITIVE curve balls you can think of that might happen to you.

3. Talk about these potential opportunities with your key stakeholders.

4. Ask yourself if there is anything that would make you pass up the opportunity of your dreams.

5. Ask yourself if there is anything you could do ahead of time to be nimble and respond quickly if something like this were to happen to you.

6. Revisit these tips and possibilities as part of an annual process of reviewing your career.

Challenging curveballs

What about the curveballs that we all dread? The painful or difficult circumstances that throw life upside down. You can probably imagine what I mean. Examples might be our own or a loved one's illness or death. The sudden or gradual need to become a caregiver or advocate for an aging parent. Downsizing at a company that eliminates your position. Being asked to leave a job because of something that you did wrong. Being asked to leave a job even though you did nothing wrong, but because the organization wants to go in a different direction or wants someone else in your role.

CASE STUDY – James

James is a nurse manager at a large academic health center. His mother has a progressively debilitating neurologic condition and is beginning to need increasing levels of care, though she still lives at her home in another city. He is an only child and is single without children of his own. James enjoys his job and the leadership opportunities he has. He lives about 120 miles from where his mother resides. He travels to see her at least every other week when he has time off, and he is becoming aware that she needs more assistance. There is a hospital in the city where she lives, and James is confident he can find work there as a nurse, but perhaps not in the level of leadership role he has in his current position. He has been in his current role for seven years and may be in serious consideration for a nursing director role with significantly more pay and benefits in the next two years.

Questions for the Reader:

1. What do you imagine the key career decision James is facing might be?

2. What do you imagine James's answers to the Hip Pocket Questions would be?

James Speaks: I used the Hip Pocket Questions and the What Matters Most to Me exercise to determine that what matters most to me is seeing that my mother is appropriately cared for while preserving my own ability to have the resources to care for her. The key career decision I am facing is whether to move to the city where she lives, care for her in her home, and get a job there, or to move her to the city where I live and place her in an assisted living community where I can check on her regularly while keeping my own job. I suppose I could put her in assisted living in her city, but if I'm going to do that, it would make more sense to me to stay in my hometown and keep my job and the opportunities it will offer.

James's Outcome: James and his mother decided that she would move to the city where he lives and works. She entered an assisted living facility, and James was able to check on her several days a week, and more frequently as her condition deteriorated. He was able to successfully compete for the new leadership position, which offered him a higher salary and a bit more flexibility in his schedule to be able to attend to his mother's needs.

This is truly an example of a challenging curveball. These are situations most of us hope to avoid, but in my years spent as an executive and leadership coach, I have seen that most people encounter at least one such episode in their careers. When this happens, I first work with clients to create a plan to survive the challenge, whatever that looks like. And then, we work to find a way for them to move forward, heal as best they can, and eventually get back to thriving.

So how do you do that exactly and can you plan for it? My tips for preparing for challenges like these are very similar to the tips for positive curveballs:

1. Keep your Hip Pocket Question responses up to date.

2. Make a list of all the CHALLENGING curveballs you can think of that you might encounter.

3. Talk about these potential challenges ahead of time with your key stakeholders.

4. Ask yourself if there is anything you could do to pre-empt any of those challenging curveballs. Can any of them be prevented or at least made less likely?

5. Ask yourself if there is anything you could do ahead of time to be nimble and respond quickly if something like this happened to you.

6. Revisit these potential issues as part of an annual process of reviewing your career.

World events as curveballs

Recall that the 9/11 attacks were a seminal moment in my own career, when I guided an entire class of students through the personal reckoning they experienced in that time of crisis. Societal crisis and change always affects people in unexpected ways, and the ripples across sectors of all types can be dramatic. Globally, we are still feeling the ripple effects of the COVID-19 pandemic. The loss of life alone during the crisis phases of the pandemic will be with us forever, but the pandemic also strained our social fabric and dealt repeated blows to the US and global economy. In addition, it has forever changed the way we all look at work and the choices we make about what we are willing to do to make a living.

Other global issues or world events could have similar consequences in the future—climate change, another pandemic with a more deadly pathogen, political violence and upheaval, even a global economic crisis. All you have to do is watch the news and you can imagine many scenarios that could lead you to rethink your career choices.

Curveballs like this might seem difficult to plan for, but doing so will leave you more prepared to navigate what's to come—whatever it is. Here are my tips (they will look familiar by now):

1. Keep your Hip Pocket Question responses up to date.

2. Make a list of a few global event curveballs you can think of that might occur. Don't try to list them all. Planning only requires that you think about one or two in order to consider your response when a crisis is global rather than just personal.

3. Talk about these potential challenges ahead of time with your key stakeholders.

4. Ask yourself if there is anything that you could do to help lessen the chances of any of these things happening.

5. Ask yourself if there is anything you could do ahead of time to be nimble and quickly respond the next time something of this magnitude happens.

6. Revisit these potential issues as part of an annual process of reviewing your career.

What to do with a curveball

As you can see, I use a clear formula for preparing to manage curveballs. It starts with knowing your answers to the Hip Pocket Questions. Then it moves to anticipating some of the curveballs that might come your way. From there, consider whether and how you can prepare ahead of time to ensure you are as ready as you can be. And finally, revisit this planning process on a regular basis.

As you may have noticed, I am a planner. But that doesn't mean I spend a lot of time and life energy dwelling on the bad things that could happen, nor should you. Plan as best as you can, and then see what life brings your way and rest in the security that you have a process for thinking through whatever happens. We are only human, and we can neither anticipate nor prevent every curveball. Make a plan, and live your life.

CHAPTER 5 – SUMMARY

Curveballs in life are a given. They can be positive or negative, personal or global. We can't stop them from coming, but there is a systematic way to prepare, and having a systematic plan accomplishes two things. It reduces anxiety when you anticipate the future, and it gives you a fallback process to use rather than panicking when a curveball happens in real time.

Core Concepts

- Curveballs happen to all of us. The better prepared you are, the better you will be able to navigate them.

- Curveballs can be positive opportunities or negative challenges, and they can happen at the personal level, like a death in the family, and a global level, like a pandemic.

- Considering the types of curveballs you might have to face will help you and your stakeholders think through how to respond to them, alleviate anxiety, and give you concrete action steps when they happen in real time.

- Planning for curveballs of all types should occur on at least an annual basis as part of your annual career review.

Key Takeaways

What are your Key Takeaways from this chapter? What did you learn, in your own words?

Very Next Actions

What Are Your Very Next Actions (VNAs) based on what you have learned in this chapter?

How will you begin the process of anticipating curveballs and building a plan for responding to them?

VNA #1:

VNA #2:

PART 3

Managing Change – The Career Transitions Cycle

Data from 2019 indicates that the average person will hold twelve jobs over the course of their lifetime, and up to 30 percent of the workforce can be expected to change careers or jobs each year. Employees between the ages of twenty-five and thirty-four stay in a job for a median 2.8 years, while those aged fifty-five to sixty-four will stay for a median of 9.9 years.[10] An Australian report from 2017 suggests that a fifteen-year-old at that time could expect to experience what they described as a "portfolio career" involving seventeen different jobs over five different careers during the span of their working life.[11]

---

[10] Kolmar, Chris. "Average Number of Jobs in a Lifetime [2023]: How Many Jobs Does the Average Person Have." Zippia – The Career Expert. Zippia.Com, January 11, 2023. https://www.zippia.com/advice/average-number-jobs-in-lifetime/.

[11] "The New Work Smarts: Thriving in the New Work Order." FYA_TheNewWorkSmarts_July2017.Pdf. The Foundation for Young Australians, July 1, 2017. https://www.fya.org.au/app/uploads/2021/09/FYA_TheNewWorkSmarts_July2017.pdf.

The Great Resignation,[12] which started during the height of the COVID-19 pandemic, only exacerbated the fluidity of career trajectories. This term was coined by scholar Dr. Anthony Klotz based on his review of 2020 data from the Bureau of Labor Statistics. The concept is that many people are rethinking work and their relationship to it and making career and job transition decisions accordingly. The convergence of a global crisis with the changing nature of work and business forced a shift that has been a long time coming. Our work world may never be the same. This data tells us that career transitions are happening everywhere, and a lot of people are going through them. However, I have found that few people have a framework for talking about this process, and fewer still can help mentor someone else through it. I hope to change that.

This section is all about the process of managing career transition, the second pillar of the Professional Careers by Design™ approach. We will examine why people make career transitions and I'll share some tools to help you know whether it's time to make a change, and then we will take a deep dive into the *how* of career transitions. That's where you'll learn about the Career Transitions Cycle—a roadmap for moving through a career transition, and a framework that has yielded great success for me and my clients. I hope to help you understand career changes as a series of steps or stages that occur in a relatively predictable fashion, whether you are in your first transition or your tenth. Along the way, I'll describe the stages of transition and what you should be thinking about and accomplishing as part of each stage.

It is important to know that this cycle is NOT linear. People can go "forward" and "backward" on the path many times before actually completing a job transition. If you are considering multiple possible jobs, each

---

[12] Cohen, Arianne. "How to Quit Your Job in the Great Post-Pandemic Resignation Boom." *Bloomberg Business Week* (New York), May 10, 2021. https://www.bloomberg.com/news/articles/2021-05-10/quit-your-job-how-to-resign-after-covid-pandemic#xj4y7vzkg.

one may be at a different stage of this process. That's OK. This roadmap will still work for you. The idea is simply to have a way of planning and implementing your career transition, and managing the tremendous amount of work, information, and emotion that goes with it.

Let's jump in.

Career Transitions – Key Concepts

Why Do We Make Career Transitions?

Peeople make career changes for myriad reasons. As we discussed in Section 2 of this book, there are personal, family, organizational, and industry reasons for change, as well as positive and challenging curveballs that can be personal or global.

When my clients have sorted out their answers to the Hip Pocket Questions, we determine if they are best served by staying put and building new skills and relationships or by leaving for something new. If there is no urgent personal or professional circumstance creating a need for immediate change (such as a layoff), our next step is typically an exercise that I call the Four Es of Your Career Evolution. This tool is really a lens for exploring and answering this question: **Do you still have more to learn, do, or experience where you are? Or have you done all you can do?** If the latter is the case, it might be time for some kind of change. If it is the former, you will be looking for ways to continue to grow and thrive where you are.

The Four Es

The Four Es—Education, Experience, Exposure, and Enthusiasm—serve as a helpful lens for assessing your current professional situation and can help you think about opportunities that come your way. It may help to think a little hypothetically. It is probably clear why you would leave a bad job. If you are unfairly compensated, experiencing a toxic workplace relationship, or otherwise mistreated, the decision can be extremely clear-cut. But what about a reasonably good job? Why would you leave, and what would you want next? And if you were to decide to stay, what would make you do that? Reasons to choose a job from among the possibilities available to you include:

1. Education: you are learning a new skill, concept, culture, or other valuable material.

2. Experience: you are gaining experience in a company, in a certain job or role, or at a particular level of leadership.

3. Exposure: you are being seen in a new way by key stakeholders in your career, particularly those who can help you advance.

4. Enthusiasm: you have a deep passion for your work, and it has meaning for you.

These are key ways in which your current job might be enhancing your career, and they are also key reasons that a new role might be worthy of consideration. They don't all need to happen at once, although that would certainly be nice, and some may be more important to you than others (to decide, go back to your list of what matters most to you). However, they will help you clarify whether you are still getting something out of your current circumstances.

Putting the Four Es into Practice

I urge clients to look at their current circumstances through the lens of each of the Four Es, and then to determine what they are and are not getting out of their job.

Suppose you've lost your enthusiasm but are still gaining exposure or learning skills you will need in the future. That has value and may be reason enough to stay. If you've not gotten a lot of exposure but still feel a deep passion for what you do, that may also have value for you and be reason enough to stay. What if none of the Four Es are happening for you? Perhaps it's time for a change. The change you make could be a new job, but it could also involve a change in your existing job. If you feel you've done all the learning you can do but it's not a great time to make a big move, consider asking for new assignments or learning opportunities. These can be framed around your long-term goals. For example, if you know your eventual goal is to be a department chair but you have no budgeting experience, ask about how you can get this kind of knowledge with a new project or assignment. It's all about making a strategic decision that works for you now and in the future.

If you ultimately decide it is time to move on, the Four Es can also guide your next step. What is most important to you in a new job? This can guide your search, the questions you ask during the vetting process, and the decision you make after an offer is extended.

Deciding Whether to Stay or Go

Recall that in Chapter 4, I described the final step in the five-step process as "Make a Decision." The core question for that step is either:

"How do you want to learn and grow from a place where you are currently thriving?" OR

"What are you ready, willing, and able to do about any misalignments you have identified?"

Sometimes clients need a little help getting to their answer. They may even need a little help determining which question they should be asking. That's where the Stay/Go Grid comes in. It centers around this question: Should I stay, or should I go?

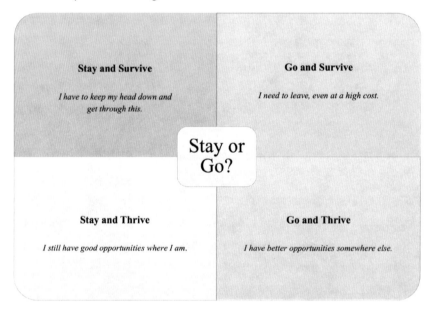

Stay and Survive	**Go and Survive**
I have to keep my head down and get through this.	*I need to leave, even at a high cost.*
Stay or Go?	
Stay and Thrive	**Go and Thrive**
I still have good opportunities where I am.	*I have better opportunities somewhere else.*

Figure 3: The Stay-Go Grid

As you can see, it is a simple tool that boils your circumstances down into four categories. The grid lays out the choices of "stay vs. go" and "survive vs. thrive," creating four quadrants, each of which has its own opportunities and challenges.

Determining which quadrant you are in starts with a deep dive into what you are getting out of your job, role, and institution. Understanding which of the Four Es (as described above), if any, you are enjoying in your current role will help you see whether you are surviving and thriving. Meanwhile, a landscape scan and a clear sense of which of the Four Es you need most will help clarify whether you can thrive by staying or whether you must go to do so.

Ultimately, finding your place on the grid will link back to what matters most to you, and it might explain why someone would choose "stay and survive" over "go and thrive." Let's look at each of the scenarios described in the Stay/Go Grid.

Stay and survive

This quadrant probably doesn't sound pleasant, but staying and surviving does not have to mean misery or stagnation—and there may be good reasons to make this choice. Suppose your youngest child is finishing college and you want to start a business but need to stay on salary while you still have a tuition bill to pay. Or maybe you're close but not quite vested in the corporate retirement plan. Perhaps you are bored with your current assignments, but you'd love a shot at your supervisor's job when she retires in a year. These are all reasons you might stay and bide your time. In this situation, growth is not necessarily your primary aim. That doesn't mean you can't grow, but your decision to stay is motivated by something else in the short term. This is a lot like the idea of leaning out during difficult life circumstances as opposed to leaning in (described by Sheryl Sandberg in her book on the topic).[13] If your focus needs to be elsewhere beyond your career, that's just fine.

Go and survive

This set of circumstances is not an easy place to be. If staying and surviving is not tenable, you have no choice but to go. Layoffs, toxic relationships, pay cuts, and other challenges can all land someone in the "go and survive" quadrant. If you find yourself in this situation, your best bet is to determine

---

[13] Sandberg, Sheryl. 2013. *Lean In: Women, Work and the Will to Lead*. New York: Knopf.

what surviving and thriving would each look like, then use that as a lens for assessing opportunities. What do you need most out of your next position? Start with Maslow's Hierarchy of Needs.[14] You likely need a paycheck that will get you the basics. What about your other needs? How far up the hierarchy you can go will depend on your personal situation, what you learn from your landscape scan, and which of the Four Es is most meaningful to you. With luck and a clear understanding of these considerations, "go and survive" can turn into "go and thrive."

Stay and thrive

If you land in "stay and thrive," it's because you are still getting some value out of your current work. It aligns with what matters most to you and is also giving you at least one of the 4 Es. You are learning new things (getting an education), developing experience, gaining exposure, or enjoying enthusiasm in the current situation. If that's the case, staying is a way to thrive. It's important, however, to check in with yourself every few months or when you've had a major life change to ensure your needs have not changed. If you are no longer getting any of the 4 Es, you might have slipped from "stay and thrive" to "stay and survive." You may still choose to stay, but it's important to revisit the stay/go question in case it's time for something new.

Go and thrive

This quadrant is about seeing opportunity elsewhere and seizing it. Often (but not always), this is where people land after a period of "stay and survive." To find your "thrive" opportunity, revisit your list of what matters most to you. Again, determine which of the Four Es you want out of your

---

[14] Maslow, Abraham H. "A Theory of Human Motivation." *Psychological Review 50*, no. 4 (1943): 370-396. Accessed June 25, 2023. https://doi.org/https://psycnet.apa.org/doi/10.1037/h0054346.

next role, and then go for it. Once you've made the leap and are thriving in your new environment, you won't regret your choice.

Should you stay, or should you go?

When clients are considering this question, I ask if they have a gut feeling about it and why. The Stay/Go Grid helps us give context to that gut feeling. It's also useful once we've determined where someone has landed because each portion of the grid has a set of skills to be focusing on. No matter where you land, there are things you can do to continue supporting your own career development, even if it's not time for the job of your dreams.

It is also a good idea to understand what I call your "bright red lines"—the factors that will push you from stay to go, for example. These could be moral and ethical considerations, or they could involve something like schedule inflexibility. What would make a tenable situation untenable, and vice versa? All these thought processes will help you understand if you're in the right quadrant for you … and what it will take to change your situation if you're not.

So, what about the question we started with—should you stay, or should you go? It's up to you, your priorities, and needs. But using these tools will help you find clarity, and ultimately your best answer for this season of your life.

Overview of The Career Transitions Cycle

Do you recall this quiz from Chapter 3? I asked you to determine where you are in your career transition journey. Take a moment and refresh your memory about which description fits your current situation the best.

A.   I am in a job that I am happy and content with. I'm not considering any changes to my career at all.

B. Something has happened (good or bad) that has made me start thinking about a career change.

C. I am actively searching for a new opportunity. I've submitted applications or letters of interest, or I'm interviewing for new positions.

D. I am negotiating terms for one or more new positions. I've received at least one offer and am negotiating terms for those positions while still in my current job.

E. I'm in an active transition between jobs. I have a new position I'm headed for and trying to wrap up my current role.

F. I am in a new job and trying to figure out how to succeed.

Make a note of the letter for your choice. You'll want to refer to it as we go through the next several chapters. Each of these descriptions fits a specific stage of what I call the Career Transitions Cycle. Now that you have done some of the basic work of crafting an intentionally designed career, I want to take you a bit deeper. The rest of this section of the book describes the Career Transitions Cycle and provides you with the tools you need to put it into practice in your own life.

The stages correspond to the letters of your response in the quiz above, so pay special attention to where you fit into this cycle. Here are the stages of the Career Transitions Cycle:

Stage 1: Happy and Thriving—you are in a new or stable position and not considering any changes.

Stage 2: Search Targeting—you have decided that you need to consider a move, and you are trying to figure out the details of what you might be looking for.

Stage 3: Search to Offer—you are actively involved in one or more searches, crafting letters of intent, polishing your resume or CV, and preparing for or participating in interviews. You may be working with search committees or search firms in this stage.

Stage 4: Negotiation—you have at least one offer for a new role or position, and you are actively negotiating the terms of that offer.

Stage 5: Offboarding and Onboarding—you have accepted an offer for a new role or position, perhaps in the same organization or maybe in a different one. You are leaving one position behind and getting ready to take on another.

Stage 6: Setting Yourself up for Success—you have nearly or fully completed the offboarding process and are beginning to assume the duties of your new role. You hope to make a great first impression and learn the ropes of the new role and institution, although it's possible your employer has not changed, and you are working to build healthy relationships with those you supervise, work with, and report to.

Figure 4: The Career Transitions Cycle

It is important to remember that you will move back and forth between these stages throughout your career, and if you are planning a transition, there is no fixed amount of time you are likely to spend in each stage. If you have multiple jobs or career directions to consider, each one of those potential transitions could be in a different stage at the same time. You can see why a roadmap will be helpful. The next chapters will explore each of these stages in more detail, giving you the roadmap you'll need to thrive through all of them.

CHAPTER 6 TOOL

Purpose of the exercise

Sometimes it can be confusing to discern whether it's actually time to leave a job, or whether you would be better off staying, and what your reasons are for making the choice. The Stay-Go Grid is a tool to help you figure out which choice is right for you at this time and in your current circumstances.

Instructions

Use this table to describe what each of the career options below might look like for you. Include the Very Next Action (VNA) steps that would be needed to see that choice through, and the pros and cons of that choice. Determine which quadrant of this grid seems to fit you best. Also include any other notes that might help you discern the best next steps for you.

Stay and Survive	**Go and Survive**
I have to keep my head down and get through this.	*I need to leave, even at a high cost.*
What is my VNA?	What is my VNA?
What are the pros of this approach?	What are the pros of this approach?
What are the cons of this approach?	What are the cons of this approach
Stay or Go?	
Stay and Thrive	**Go and Thrive**
I still have good opportunities where I am.	*I have better opportunities somewhere else.*
What is my VNA?	What is my VNA?
What are the pros of this approach?	What are the pros of this approach?
What are the cons of this approach?	What are the cons of this approach

Notes about the choice before you:

CHAPTER 6 SUMMARY

This chapter provides you with the tools you'll need for considering the why, whether, and how of career transitions, and they will prove useful throughout your career. Use them as often as necessary to keep your career transitions grounded in your values, what matters most to you, and the circumstances in which you find yourself.

Core Concepts

- People make transitions in their careers for a variety of reasons.

- The Four Es can help inform your thinking about WHY you might be ready for a transition.

- The Stay-Go Grid can help you decide WHETHER it's time to stay or go in your current role.

- The Career Transitions Cycle will help you understand HOW to make a transition.

Key Takeaways

What are your Key Takeaways from this chapter? What did you learn, in your own words?

Very Next Actions

After reading this chapter, are there any Very Next Actions (VNAs) you need to take based on what you have learned?

VNA #1:

VNA #2:

Career Transition Stage 1 –
Happy and Thriving

The stage I call "Happy and Thriving" is one where you have typically just started a new role or have been in the role a while and are very satisfied. You have good work-life alignment, your work is meaningful to you, and while you know a change may come at some point, you likely don't have a plan or a timeline for that change to happen. You might think, "I don't need to think about leaving yet. I don't want to jinx anything, and I don't want anyone to think I'm not happy." Your family may not want to hear any consideration of change, particularly if you have recently transitioned into your role. Folks in this stage just want to stay put, and usually for very good reasons.

Believe it or not, it's still worth monitoring your place on the career roadmap. Although I'm not advocating that you start planning your exit just as you walk in the door at a new job, I have seen in my work with clients that people benefit when they consistently consider how they want to grow. Planning for that growth is the way we bring intentionality to that discussion.

If you are new to your role, you may be asking yourself about new skills and relationships the position requires. Is this a "stretch assignment" for you, meaning you need to gain and start using a new skill quickly? You'll need to plan for that. Similarly, you'll want to invest time in the relationships you'll need to be successful. Who are the key people in the organization that are new to you, or with whom you have a new relationship? How do they make decisions, and how do they communicate about those decisions? What can you learn from them about their preferred styles of leadership and managing information? You'll also want to consider anyone you are supervising—what matters most to them? What do they need to do their jobs? How do they receive and use information from you, and how do they interact with the organization?

All these things are useful to learn as you onboard, and they will ultimately help you be more successful. Take advantage of your relative sense of newness and gather information about how you and others around you can thrive. If you have been in your role for a while and are very fulfilled, what is happening in your environment? In your industry? Are there new technologies or approaches you need to keep up with? Are there leadership skills you would like to learn? If you are not already in a "stretch assignment," how can you get involved with a project that will teach you something new and make it apparent to others that you are building your skills? Is there a degree, advanced training, or a course you would like to pursue to learn something new? Who are the key people in the organization who can influence your career, and how can you connect with them or nurture that relationship?

Mentorship is a rewarding part of this stage and one that people who are happy and thriving will have time and mental bandwidth to pursue. Is there anyone in the organization you would like to mentor? Anyone who might be a successor for you when you are ready to move on from your current role? Devoting your time and energy to the mentoring process can enhance your sense of thriving and can offer others around you a path to their own leadership growth and development.

Asking yourself where you want to focus your energy and time during this stage can build on that sense you have that you are thriving, and help you continue to feel fresh and new in a situation you enjoy.

Although this is a stage of the Career Transitions Cycle, it is less about change or transition and more about growth. Growth of skills, talents, visibility. Think of the Four Es— education, experience, exposure, and enthusiasm. Is there anything in that list you want to focus on that will move you toward growth, even while you are feeling great about where you are?

CHAPTER 7 TOOL

Purpose of the exercise

As you consider whether it's time to change jobs, take on a new role, or figure out a good reason for staying in your current role or situation, this worksheet will help you make your decision by considering four key attributes that bring meaning and fulfillment to any job:

- **Education** – you are LEARNING a new skill, concept, culture or other valuable material.
- **Experience** – you are gaining EXPERIENCE in a company, in a certain job or role, or at a particular level of leadership.
- **Exposure** – you are being SEEN in a new way by key stakeholders in your career, particularly those who can help you advance.
- **Enthusiasm** – you have a deep PASSION for your work, and it has MEANING for you.

It's good to inventory where you stand as you start a new job, when you consider leaving your current job and as you plan a search. The Four Es will help.

Instructions

Answer the questions below about the CURRENT STATE and the DESIRED STATE of your career. Use what you learn to develop your key takeaways from this exploration, then rate your likelihood of seeking a career transition at the present time. Use what you learned to develop three Very Next Actions (VNAs) that will help you move forward.

CURRENT STATE

In my current role or career situation, what am I gaining with regard to the Four Es?

- Education – What am I learning?

- Experience – How am I building on my professional skillset?

- Exposure – How am I gaining visibility in my organization or in my profession?

- Enthusiasm – What parts of my work ignite my passion and give meaning to my life?

WHAT ARE MY KEY TAKEAWAYS ABOUT THE CURRENT STATE OF MY CAREER?

The Four Es
Page 2

DESIRED STATE

When I am ready to make a career transition, what should I be looking for?

- Education – What new skills, concepts or cultures do I want to learn about?

- Experience – What experience do I want to gain next that will build my professional
- skills and help advance my career?

- Exposure – How might a new job enhance my professional visibility?

- Enthusiasm – What passion and meaning am I seeking through my work?

WHAT ARE MY KEY TAKEAWAYS ABOUT THE DESIRED STATE OF MY CAREER?

LIKELIHOOD RATING FOR CAREER TRANSITION

Given my CURRENT STATE and my DESIRED STATE, how likely is it that I am ready to seek a career transition RIGHT NOW? Circle the number that best represents your assessment today.

1 = I AM VERY HAPPY IN MY CURRENT STATE   5 = I NEED TO MAKE A TRANSITION

1   2   3   4   5

The Four Es - Page 3

GIVEN WHAT I HAVE LEARNED FROM THIS EXERCISE, WHAT ARE MY VERY NEXT ACTIONS (VNAs) FOR MY CAREER AT THIS TIME? List at least three VNAs you think would help you move forward.

1.

2.

3.

NOTES:

CHAPTER 7 – SUMMARY

Being happy and thriving is a good thing. Not all situations require a transition of career, role, or organization. If you are in this stage, focus on growth rather than change.

Core Concepts

- Consider new skills you want to gain or practice. Seek stretch assignments or tasks that will help you grow those skills.

- Consider relationships you want to build or nurture. Use your time in this stage to grow the base of your network.

- Revisit the Four Es—is there anything from that list you want to grow or enhance?

- Consider whether there is anyone in your organization whom you want to mentor, or even help to develop as a future successor for your role when you move on. It's never too early to plan for succession.

Key Takeaways

What are your Key Takeaways from this chapter? What did you learn, in your own words?

Very Next Actions

After reading this chapter, are there any Very Next Actions (VNAs) you need to take based on what you have learned?

VNA #1:

VNA #2:

Career Transitions Stage 2 – Search Targeting

At this point, you have decided that you either want or need to look at new opportunities. You may not be certain what is available to you or what you want, and that's OK. This is a good time to assess the things that matter most to you. It's also a time to ask what you want out of your work life. What does your ideal job and work life look like? Who will be affected by the decisions you make? Does your ideal job exist in the marketplace, or will you need to create such a position, either in your own business, or by influencing an organization to create a job like that for you? Where might such a position be located geographically? Where are you and those you care about willing to live? Are there places you would LOVE to live, or places you would like to avoid? Answering these questions can help you target your search so that you zero in on the work and work life you want in a place you'd like to live.

The Reporter's Questions

I often meet clients when they are in this stage of the Career Transitions Cycle, and I encourage them to focus on four questions, in this order:

1. **Where** do I want to look?

2. **What** kind of job am I looking for?

3. **Who** might have this kind of job in the geographic areas I am considering?

4. **When** do I want to start the search process?

Eventually there will be a fifth question, "How will I get there?" That question gets answered in Part 4 of this book. For now, you might recognize these as the classic journalist's questions of who, what, where, when, why, and how. I want to take a moment to give a shout-out to David W. Brewer, PhD, a mentor and friend of mine since the day I began medical school. Dave taught me, over many years of guidance about my career, to face each career choice with these five questions. They have been a great framework for my own career explorations, and I must give Dave the credit and my deepest gratitude for giving me permission to share them with you.[15]

Where?

When a client with whom I am working enters the search targeting phase, I ask him to consider geography first. Here is my geographic questions checklist:

- Why might you need to stay in or move to a particular geographic location (for example, children who need to complete a portion of their schooling or a family member who requires your presence for caregiving)?

- What areas of the country (or the world, if you are adventurous) have you always dreamt of living in?

- What areas of the country or the world are you absolutely certain are locations where you do not want to live? If there are places on this list, I typically suggest that you make a list of the reasons for

---

[15] Brewer, David W. *Personal Conversation (Electronic Permission Granted and on File)* (Carbondale, IL), August 15, 1983.

eliminating a particular location. The reasons may be sound, and they may not change, but occasionally I meet someone for whom a decision to avoid a particular location is based on reasons that no longer make sense. Just pausing to ask the question sometimes opens opportunities to consider that location anew.

Once people have asked these questions, I encourage them to do what I call the "Map Exercise." Buy a map of the country or the world, depending on the scope of your search targeting. The map should be big enough to hang on the wall and mark on. Choose two different colored markers and circle all the places where you might really love or at least be willing to live in one color. Make an "X" in the second color over any places you are absolutely certain you do not want to live. Then, if you have stakeholders, such as a spouse or older children you want to include in this exercise, ask them to do the same. Look for the overlaps in geography. The areas where there is some agreement about places you are collectively willing to look are the first places to *target* as you begin your search.

What?

When you are ready to ask, "What kind of job am I looking for," you may already have a pretty good idea of the answer, particularly if you have been following the career design processes I outlined in Parts 1 and 2 of this book. If you're not quite there, try the process I walk through with clients:

- Review your Hip Pocket Questions list to see if you have current and accurate answers for this season of your life.

- Review any opportunities that have come your way—look back at that "Positive Curveballs" list from Chapter 5.

- Review the Four Es list—what do you want or need from your next job?

Who?

When you have considered these questions, go back to the map from the exercise above. Now ask yourself these questions:

- Who (employers, institutions, companies) might have a job that fits the parameters you are looking for in the geographic areas you are considering?

- Are those employers hiring right now?

- Do you know anyone at one or more of those organizations who might help you explore opportunities?

- Does anyone you know have a connection with someone else at one or more of those organizations, particularly someone who makes hiring decisions?

- Is this a job you need to *create* for yourself, either by convincing someone in an organization to create it with you in mind, or by starting your own business to meet a need in the marketplace and make your ideal job happen?

If you have a connection with any of the organizations you identify, you can leverage those or make contact directly to learn more. If there are position descriptions available for opportunities you may wish to target, gather them. Begin to do your due diligence by finding out more about the employers and the locations in which you find them. Are the organizations stable? Is the location desirable? Does the position meet your professional and personal needs for growth and progression in your intentionally designed career?

Don't forget to ask yourself whether YOU might be the employer of choice for this stage in your career. Are you entrepreneurial? Do you have skills and talents that might be needed in the marketplace? Do you have any desire to run your own business and the resources to take that step? I bring this up here because occasionally, someone reaches this stage of the Career Transitions Cycle and says something to me like, "The best boss on the planet for me at this stage of my life and career is ME!" That's when it becomes time to explore the entrepreneurial part of the pathway, described in Chapter 13.

When?

Once you have gathered the information and answered the questions already laid out in this chapter, it's time to think about timing. Consider:

- Is there a cyclical nature to when employers hire for the kinds of jobs that I'm seeking (do they hire at the beginning of a fiscal or academic year, at the start of a grant cycle, as the legislature provides funding, or some other process that will influence the timing of when you should apply)?

- Is there anything in my life that would interfere with my ability to start and participate in a search process? Pursuing a new role does take intellectual, physical, and emotional work, and it takes time. When are you going to be ready for the next phase of the Career Transitions Cycle? When can you apply for jobs and start interviewing? There may never be a perfect time, but you'll want to be sure you're ready to devote the time and energy the next step will require.

Is There Anything Else You Need to Know?

At this point, you likely have a pretty good idea of one (or hopefully several) potential targets for your search. You may have a clear connection to someone who is making a hiring decision, and hopefully you have some position descriptions to review. I suggest one more set of considerations:

- What else do you need to know to get started on your search? Who do you know who might have information that would be useful?

- What is your ideal timeline? Map it out.

- Are you applying for one position at a time, or several at the same time? There are good reasons to consider each approach, and the best answer for you will be unique to your situation.

I suggest you spend some time on these questions, so that you create a period of reflection before you dive into your search process. That's when things will really get interesting—and busy. The preparation from this chapter will help you be ready for the sprint when you get there.

CHAPTER 8 TOOL

Search Targeting Checklist

Purpose of the exercise

This exercise is designed to help you consider the questions that will help you get ready to launch a job search.

Instructions

Answer the questions below for yourself, and discuss them with your key stakeholders.

 Where do my stakeholders and I want to be geographically?

- Why might you need to stay in or move to a particular geographic location (for example, children who need to complete a portion of their schooling or a family member who requires your presence for caregiving)?
- What areas of the country (or the world, if you are adventurous) have you always dreamed of living in or exploring?
- What areas of the country or the world are you absolutely certain you do not want to live?

 What kind of job do I want at this stage of my career?

- Review your Hip Pocket Questions list to see if you have current and accurate answers for THIS SEASON of your life.
- Review any opportunities that have come your way – look back at that "Positive Curveballs" list from Chapter 5.
- Review the Four E's – what do you want or need from your next job?

Search Targeting Checklist
Page 2

 Who might have jobs that meet my needs in my preferred location?

- Who (what employers, institutions, companies) might have a job that fits the parameters you are looking for in geographic areas you are considering?
- Are those employers hiring right now?
- Do you know anyone at one or more of those organizations who might help you explore opportunities?
- Does anyone you know have a connection at one or more of those organizations, particularly someone who makes hiring decisions?
- Would YOU be the best boss for you – are you willing, ready and able to explore becoming an entrepreneur?

 What, if anything, else should I be considering?

- What else do you need to know to get started on your search? Who do you know who might have information that would be useful?
- What is your ideal timeline? Map it out.
- Are you applying for one position at a time, or several at the same time? There are good reasons to consider each approach, and the best answer for you will be unique to your situation.

NOTES:

CHAPTER 8 – SUMMARY

The activities of the Search Targeting Stage of the Career Transitions Cycle will help you sort through a wide range of questions about what kind of position will help advance your Designed Career and where you want to be. Working through these questions will also help you sort and plan for the time and energy needed as you begin the next stage of implementing your search strategy.

Core Concepts

- There are four sets of questions to consider in the Search Targeting stage of the Career Transitions Cycle:

- **Where** do I want to look?

- **What** kind of job am I seeking?

- **Who** might have this kind of job in the geographic areas I am considering?

- **When** do I want to start the search process?

- Systematically working through these questions will allow you to focus on the opportunities that are worth your time and energy as you move into the next stage of the cycle.

Key Takeaways

What are your Key Takeaways from this chapter? What did you learn, in your own words?

Very Next Actions

After reading this chapter, are there any Very Next Actions (VNAs) you need to take based on what you have learned?

VNA #1:

VNA #2:

9

Career Transition Stage 3 –
Search to Offer

By the time you reach this stage, you are likely ready to submit an application or letter of interest for a position you have targeted, or perhaps you are considering a new position based on someone targeting YOU. You are probably asking yourself what skills you should highlight in your resume or curriculum vitae. You may be wondering what the organizations you have focused on are looking for in a candidate and how you can craft a cover letter that tells your story well. What is the narrative story line of your career that makes it clear you are a great fit?

You may also be working with a search firm and asking yourself how to navigate that process. What do you tell the search consultant? For whom does the search consultant work, and how involved is he in the process? You will probably have questions about the interview and selection process, including timeline and who will actually make the hiring decision. Planning for interviews is a key part of this stage, so anticipating the questions you might be asked and preparing questions for you to ask the interviewers yourself will be important.

Deciding when to tell your current employer that you are actively searching for a new position is another consideration—one that depends on timing. All these issues relate to core steps in the process of actively searching for a new job, and we will explore them all. This is a BUSY stage, and if you are actively engaged in more than one search at the same time, it can get especially complicated. Let's break it down into a manageable set of steps:

- Staying Organized
- Getting Advice Along the Way
- Telling Your Story
  - Updating your resume or curriculum vitae
  - Tailoring your narrative for a cover letter
- Working with the Deciders
  - Search firms and search consultants
  - Search committees and "deciders"
- Interviews—A Two-Way Street
- Receiving an Offer
- Communicating about the Search Process

Staying Organized

Search to Offer is such a complex and busy part of the Career Transitions Cycle that staying organized is a major task. I encourage people to either use a spreadsheet or an electronic task manager to track each search process that they enter. Whether you make a spreadsheet or use some other tool to guide you, what's important is that you have all the contact information in front of you in one place. You'll want to track when and with whom you have communicated and identify the Very Next Action you need to take for each role you are seeking. Keep this information readily accessible for review. Following up on those VNAs on a weekly or biweekly basis can help you meet deadlines, and it will help relieve some of your anxiety about the process.

Getting Advice Along the Way

This period will be stressful, and most people benefit from having a trusted advisor to help guide them along the way. This should be someone outside the search process and probably someone outside your current institution unless you trust the person to maintain your confidentiality. I've seen search candidates work with a trusted mentor or colleague, and this kind of relationship is often very helpful. Whomever you choose, look to someone who knows you, your field, and perhaps even the organization you are applying to as well as your current employer. If you do not have access to such a mentor or colleague, it's worth considering using a Search Coach. Professional coaches who specialize in helping people navigate the complexities of the job search process can be particularly helpful in this stage of a career transition. My advice is to seek a coach who knows your industry, who has experience coaching people in positions similar to those you are seeking, and who has professional training and credentialing as a coach. You can expect to pay for this service, but I believe coaching of this sort can be very helpful, and I know many professionals who believe it to be very much worth the investment.

Telling Your Story

When you have selected the target position for your search, the biggest hurdle—the one that causes the most anxiety, and the one that causes people to stall—is writing your cover letter and updating your resume or curriculum vitae. Let's walk through what you need to know.

Curriculum Vitae or Résumé—Which One Should You Use?

There is a fundamental difference between the types of documents most commonly used in a job search. For professional and academic positions, the expectation is typically that you will submit a curriculum vitae, while for most business and corporate positions, the expectation is more common that you will submit a résumé. So, what's the difference?

A curriculum vitae (Latin for "course of life" and "CV" for short) is generally a summary of your academic accomplishments as well as your training, employment history, specialized credentials, and licensure status. In academic settings, this document typically begins with education and employment history, then includes sections for **scholarly activities** (research grants, publications, presentations, and academic posters, to name a few), **teaching** (at all levels of learners), and **service** (which includes a variety of committee work, and in certain professions it includes professional service to clients). A CV generally focuses on your credentials for a job, rather than skills and competencies. The length of a CV depends upon the length of your career and experience, your accomplishments, and the expectations of the organization to which you are submitting the document, but it's not unusual for them to be thirty pages or more, depending on the length of your career and your professional accomplishments.

A résumé (French for "summary"), on the other hand, typically emphasizes your competencies, skills, and experience, and it is often limited to one to two pages. **Brevity** is a plus for a résumé, as is meeting the expectations of those who will read it, so check with others who are familiar with the organization to get a sense of how long it should be. Résumés typically include **work experience** and **key skills**, with **education and training** often listed at the end of the document, so that the focus remains on your **skills and competency** for the job that you are seeking, rather than academic or other credentials and accomplishments.

Tailoring Your CV or Résumé to the Application

It is important to note that, while you may (and probably should) maintain a "master document" with all your credentials, training, history, and accomplishments, you should tailor your CV or résumé for each position to which you apply. I advise clients to start their preparations by looking at sample documents submitted for similar positions, then reviewing the position description. Highlight all the skills, qualifications, and other elements listed in the description, so you can make sure your tailored document shows exactly how you meet or exceed their expectations for the position.

Mind the Gaps

Review your résumé or CV for any gaps. Readers of these documents are looking for unexplained gaps in your professional history, and if they see a gap, you can count on them asking you about it if you get an interview. In some cases, you may never get the chance. Some organizations use unexplained gaps to winnow applicants, so be sure this doesn't happen to you. Did you take a year off to travel in Europe, or to work in AmeriCorps or a similar nonprofit organization? Add a note explaining what you did and when. Did you take a six-month hiatus when your child was born, or when your father was ill? Explain this as well, perhaps describing the time as a "commitment to family caregiving."

Write a Great Cover Letter

The cover letter is your introduction to the people who will make decisions about hiring for this position. It's often the first thing they will see, so making an outstanding first impression is key. Develop a tailored cover letter for each position to which you apply, telling your story in a way that describes the fit among you, the organization, and the position. Here are my recommendations for doing this well:

- Tell your story. Do you remember taking English Composition or English Literature in high school, and being taught about the "narrative arc" of a story? Your letter should convey your narrative by describing how everything you have done to this point has prepared you for and led you to apply for *this* job at *this* organization at *this* time in your life.

- Begin with enthusiasm! Start your letter with a statement of your enthusiastic interest in the position, what led you to consider the role, and why you are drawn to the organization.

- Don't rehash your CV or résumé. Those documents contain a detailed inventory of your credentials, competencies, skills, and experience, so there's no need to repeat them here. Instead, use the cover letter to enhance the details and fill in the parts that are "behind the scenes" of your CV or résumé.

- Use your cover letter to describe anything unusual about your story. If your professional history has a gap, you may wish to share more about it here, such as what you learned from that time outside the normal work world. If you switched careers, discuss why and how. If you have had several positions in a relatively short period of time, describe the reasons for this, and how this experience positioned you for the job you're seeking now.

- Finish strong! Revisit your enthusiastic start and reinforce why you are a great fit for the role and the organization. Thank the reader for their time in reviewing your materials and tell them that you look forward to hearing from them about next steps.

A Note About Waiting

Sometimes people get frustrated at this point in the Search to Offer phase. It's a good idea to keep a spreadsheet tracking when you sent out each set of materials, to whom, and when you plan to follow up. Sometimes a follow-up note is appropriate within two to three weeks, but for jobs with lengthy hiring cycles, it's more likely to take a month or two before you hear anything, and the wait can be difficult.

If you have had verbal contact (by email or phone) with anyone involved in the search process, ask one of my favorite questions: "When would it be reasonable for me to expect to hear back about the next steps in your process?" Many times, you can get concrete information that will help you manage your own anxiety about the status of your application. Add anything you learn to your spreadsheet, so you can send a follow-up note at the appropriate time. Also, keep the calendar top of mind. In some environments, such as academia, summer breaks or holidays can slow the search process, and sometimes the timing for a hire may be timed to correspond with when new graduates enter the profession. That can make for a months-long wait, so don't get discouraged. Gather and record any information you can, then determine your VNA for each application and when you should act on it.

Working With the Deciders

For each position to which you have applied, it is critical to figure out who will be making the final decision about the hire. Typically, the decider will be the new hire's direct supervisor, but sometimes the final decision is made by a more senior leader with budgetary and hiring authority. Identifying the decider is an important part of your fact-finding. Let's talk about some of the key players in this process.

Search Firms and Search Consultants

For many senior positions, organizations or institutions will retain a search firm to help them make a successful hire. There are many search firms whose primary business is providing organizations with a screened and prequalified set of candidates for an important position. I say "important" because companies and institutions typically don't invest money in a search firm unless the position involves senior leadership, scarce candidates, or both. The way this works is that the hiring organization pays the search firm to develop and oversee the search process and pre-screen a potentially large pool of candidates based on the position criteria. Next, the search firm will help the organization narrow a large pool of candidates into a manageable number of people to interview so they can move forward through the process of selection, making an offer and completing the hire. A "successful" search is not just one that results in a hire but rather the hire of someone who is qualified for the role and a good fit with the organization. It's important to remember that the search firm works for and is accountable to the hiring organization.

Search consultants are the individuals who work for the search firm and oversee the search. There is usually a lead search consultant assigned to oversee the engagement and the outcome. That individual will likely be listed as the contact person for the position and may be the person to whom you will direct your cover letter, though that is not always the case. The search consultant will handle initial screening of all candidates and may have "deciding rights" about which candidates to put forward for consideration by the organization. Imagine 150 applicants submit letters of interest for a single position. The search consultant will likely screen those applicants and select twenty to thirty for the organization to consider. In that sense, the search consultant is the FIRST decider. And a key point—the search consultant will likely be very personable with you, may position himself as someone you can trust throughout the process, and may be (very often is) in fact trustworthy. Just don't forget for whom they work—it's not YOU!

Search Committees and Hiring Deciders

Not all searches utilize a search committee, but every search has an internal organizational process for selecting candidates, negotiating with the chosen candidate, making an offer, and finalizing the hire. It will be critical for you to learn as much as you can about that process. If there is a search committee, it may be small or large. It may include members of the unit in which the hired candidate will work, but I have also seen search committees intentionally include people who will *not* have a direct working relationship with the new hire. Sometimes people who will be direct reports of the new hire are intentionally excluded from participation in the search committee. This is unusual but it does occur. More typically, there will be a mix of people from the unit, people in similar positions around the organization and people whose work will directly be affected by the person in this role.

Contrary to what you might expect, the hiring decision-maker is typically not included on the search committee. Search committees are generally tasked with sorting through a large pool of candidates, conducting a multi-stage process that includes screening, interviewing, and checking references for candidates. The final task of the search committee is typically to refer the top one to three candidates to the hiring decider, who will conduct her or his own interviews and who makes the final choice.

Interviews—A Two-Way Street

The interview process makes a lot of people nervous. If you've had a successful career and are applying for a leadership role, you may not have been on a job interview in years. When I speak with clients who find themselves in this situation, they tell me they are unsure how to present themselves, and they often feel unprepared and unable to anticipate the questions they'll be asked. In this section, I'll offer my best coaching advice about interviews.

Understand the Interview Process

First and foremost, remember that the interview—and the entire search process, for that matter—is really a two-way information-sharing process. Yes, the organization is assessing you and your qualifications and fit for the job. However, you are also assessing the position, the people with whom you might be working, and the organization. You are there to get the information you need to make the very best decision for you. The hiring organization (and the associated search firm and search consultant, if one is being employed) will be asking you questions about your experience, qualifications, successes, and challenges. It is possible (and advisable) to prepare for these questions. You should also prepare a list of your own questions for the organization. Your list of the ten things that matter most to you, which you may have created after reading Chapter 1 of this book, is a good place to start formulating your questions, and you should review it before every interview, so you stay focused on the things you care about. You'll also want to review what matters to your stakeholders, so you can be sure questions they care about get answered too.

You can typically expect to have at least one screening interview. This used to be called the airport interview because candidates would fly into the relevant city for the interview, which would take place at a hotel near the airport, so that candidates were not seen on campus and their confidentiality would not be compromised before they were willing to be identified as a candidate outside their home institution. These days, the screening interview is often conducted by videoconference, and it's used to help winnow down the pool of candidates to a manageable number for the next step. Typically, three to five candidates may be selected to move forward, though the number varies.

The second interview is typically held at the primary workplace for the organization, although in the pandemic, this step, too, started to occur via videoconference. In your second interview, you may meet with some of the same individuals, perhaps in small-group settings, or you may even meet with people one-to-one. There may also be new faces outside the search committee who will meet with and interview you. Typically, this process will yield one or two finalists for the position who may move to a third round of interviewing that sometimes includes an invitation to bring their families. Discussions of salary or of other parameters for a potential offer are typically not brought up until near the end of this third interview, and in some cases these discussions are left until the next phase. You will need to watch for cues regarding when to bring up these issues. If you simply can't get a read on this, it is reasonable to ask a question like, "At what point in your process would it be appropriate for me to inquire about the details of the position, salary, and benefits?"

Another important tip—it is not only acceptable but also highly advisable to ask a question at the end of each interview such as, "What is a reasonable expectation about when I might hear whether I have progressed in the search and hiring process? And is there a designated point of contact if I have further questions or would like to follow up?" I coach job candidates to never leave a round of interviews without asking that question because it provides clarity and helps them plan their Very Next Action.

Preparing for Your Opening Statement

Most interviews for professional positions will begin by asking the candidate to present a brief (usually five minutes or less) opening statement about themselves. This is the most important five minutes in any search process. It is your chance to make your first (and often lasting) impression. My advice is to practice ahead of time (and time yourself, so you stay within the parameters you are given), have some notes with you, and tell your story succinctly. Your opening statement should serve as an extended elevator speech about yourself, but don't spend too much time in the details covered by your CV or résumé and your cover letter. Instead, briefly touch on highlights from each, but focus primarily on connecting and conveying who you are as a candidate. Each of the three pieces of information about you should augment, with minimal duplication, one another. Think of it like this:

- Your CV or résumé gives the technical details about your credentials, skills, and employment history relevant to the position. The CV is akin to an encyclopedia. Don't reiterate it in your cover letter.

- Your cover letter or letter of interest summarizes your enthusiasm for the role, the reasons your history makes you a great fit (this is the narrative arc of your career,) and your desire to be considered for the position. The cover letter is like a short story of who you are and why you should be considered for the job. Don't reiterate this entire letter in your opening statement.

- Your opening statement distills both of those documents into a succinct verbal presentation that conveys enthusiasm and excitement to be considered in the process. This is your chance to make an in-person "pitch" of yourself as a candidate. Focus on two or three key reasons you are a fantastic fit for this role at this time, and one or two reasons you are really excited about the possibility of landing the role. These reasons may well have appeared in your cover letter, and it's OK to reinforce them, but focus on those that are most important, and tell the story face to face, within the time you are allotted. Your opening statement is like an award speech. Brevity is critical, and first impressions are the outcome.

Planning for Interview Questions— Yours and Theirs

Once you have made it through your opening statement, you can expect three or four types of questions. I'll share some tips about this process here, and you'll find a list of common interview questions at the end of this chapter. Many search committees or interview teams will work from a list of scripted questions. Each member of the committee or team will be assigned two or three questions to ask of each candidate. There are several reasons for this approach. It helps to be sure all the questions of interest to the interviewers get covered. It also ensures all that all committee members participate actively in the process and that all candidates are asked a very similar list of baseline questions. Don't be put off by the formality of this process—this approach is intended to ensure the integrity and fairness of the search process and that the institution gathers the information needed to make a final choice.

Similarly, you should develop your own list of questions you routinely ask as part of interviews for any position you are considering. Both you and the committee can (and should) go beyond these lists of standard questions and discuss things that are unique to the situation or the people in the room, but the baseline questions will get you started and ensure important topics are not missed.

Scripted questions posed by interviewers are often predictable. They may include some or all of the following:

- What makes you want to attain this position or take on this role now?
- What is your vision for the role?
- What are the top three things you would focus on in your first six months on the job?
- Behavioral questions about specific experiences, such as career successes, challenges, difficult interpersonal relationships, and the like.

Most of my clients expect questions like the first three and find them relatively straightforward to plan for. However, the behavioral interview questions tend to make people more nervous. These are the questions that sound like, "Tell me about a time when you faced a crisis." Or, "Tell me about a professional failure you have experienced." While behavioral questions can be daunting, they are also a reasonable and expected part of the process. I typically coach people to identify three stories of successes they have experienced and three stories of things they wish had gone differently. I don't coach people to call them "failures" because the only failure is the experience from which you learned nothing. This mindset sends a great message to interviewers that you are open to learning, so as you think about things you wish had gone differently, make sure you are ready to talk about what you learned. Keep the story of what happened very brief and focus on the learning you gained.

I also coach people to not be shy when describing their success stories. It's a good idea to talk about the contributions of your team, as this demonstrates a collaborative mindset and willingness to share credit. But be sure to clearly describe the steps or actions YOU took in the process, and what you learned along the way. Own your learnings *and* your contributions.

For both success stories and challenges, I suggest using the **PARL** framework (Problem or Project, Action, Result and Learnings) framework. Talk about a **P**roblem you faced or a **P**roject you had responsibility for, describe the **A**ctions you took to solve the problem or complete the project, and the **R**esults you achieved, including at least one key **L**earning you took away from the process.

Beyond the typical scripted questions, behavioral questions, success stories, and career challenges, you can expect and plan for questions that are specific to the responsibilities of the position. These might include questions about how you would handle the budgeting process, how you would assess the functionality of your team, how you might make decisions about hiring and firing, and how you would interact with key colleagues across the organization. There is no way to predict all the questions you might be asked, but the list of my favorite interview questions at the end of this chapter will give you a place to start.

There's one more bit of planning needed to prepare you for interviewers' questions. What happens if you are asked a question you are not ready to answer? Here's my best advice. A statement like this can be a gold mine of clarity and integrity. *"I don't have enough information to give you a complete answer to that question at this time. Here is the information I believe I need to be ready to answer, and here is how I will go about obtaining that information. I'd be happy to follow up with you when I have that information."*

This statement conveys a lot about who you would be in the role for which you're being vetted: You won't be prone to giving premature answers, you understand that information gathering is necessary, you know you need a plan to do that, and you are willing to answer questions when you have the information you need.

Recall that preparing for the questions you will be asked is only part of the battle (although, admittedly, it is the more challenging part!). You need to bring your own list of questions. Some questions you might want to consider asking:

- What do you (the interviewer, representing the organization) see as the top two or three opportunities for the person who is hired into this role to make important strides for the organization?
- What do you (the interviewer) see as the top two or three challenges the person selected for this role will face?
- Who are the key partners or allies for the person in this role?
- Are there new partnerships that need to be developed?
- Are there urgent issues that need to be addressed quickly?
- If I am hired for this role, how will you know that I am successful in six months, one year, three years, or and five years?

Receiving an Offer

If all goes well, by the end of the second or third interview, you may receive an offer. This offer is usually put forward by the hiring decider, but might flow through a financial officer, a human resources representative, or a senior staffer. There may be an informal discussion of the parameters of the offer at your final interview, followed by something more formal. I encourage you to ask for a written offer in all situations, and to be clear with yourself about what would constitute a reasonable offer. The next chapter about Negotiation will help you prepare for this stage.

Once you receive an offer for one position, you may still be active in other searches, and how you communicate with any or all the involved institutions will be critical. You may want to let all institutions know that you are entertaining an offer, and it's a good idea to share when you will need to make a decision on that offer. Sometimes you can leverage an offer to move another search process along but be careful about how aggressively you use this tactic. This is a critical discussion to have with a mentor or a search coach if you are managing multiple searches.

Communicating About the Search Process

One of the most common sources of anxiety for people in a job search is determining when to tell their current employer that they are searching, or that they have advanced in a search. I share some basic principles with clients that I think serve in most situations. Here are my rules of thumb:

- It is almost always better for you to tell your current boss about your search than for her to hear about it from someone else.

- If you are asked directly about whether you are looking for another job, don't lie. But you don't need to say too much either. A generic response that can be helpful is "I'm willing to look at opportunities if the right thing comes along." This approach doesn't say whether you are looking, but it also doesn't deny or dissemble. It is rare that someone will push you to say more, but if they do, a simple, "I'm not prepared to discuss this right now" statement will typically quiet the questions—at least those directed to you. You cannot stop other people from talking, even if they are not well informed about your circumstances.

- In general, if you are invited for a second interview in a search process, that's a reasonable time to tell your boss that you are in an active search. The level of information you decide to share will depend on your relationship with your boss, but I typically favor sticking to the basics. You could say something like, "I wanted to let you know that I am under consideration for a position in another unit/organization/institution. I prefer that you hear this directly from me than from others, and I have moved forward for a second interview. If I continue to move forward, I will keep you informed, and I will work with you to manage the process professionally."

There are always exceptions to these guidelines. If you have a toxic relationship with your supervisor, the best approach may be waiting as long as possible—even until your new job is won, finalized, and the contract signed. That's rare, but sometimes it is the best approach for your own professional and psychological safety. You'll also want to think about anyone who reports to you as well as your peers. In general, I advise people not to tell their teams that they are in a search until it's clear that they are moving toward being a finalist. It's also a good idea to make sure your boss knows before you tell your team and your peers. The way you manage and stage the message around your search process takes planning, and it may differ for different groups. This is one component of the job search process where a professional coach who knows the details of your situation can be particularly helpful. You can work together to create a clear timeline and messaging plan for everyone in your orbit.

A Note about Confidentiality

People are often surprised when someone finds out that they are in a search before they are ready to talk about it. A frequent question I hear is, "I thought the search committee or search firm would keep it confidential. I asked them to protect my confidentiality in the process until I was ready to go public. Can I not expect them to respect my wishes?"

I do think it's a good idea to discuss confidentiality with the search consultant or the leader of the search committee. You can start by asking what is reasonable for you to expect regarding confidentiality. However, even if they reassure you that your privacy will be respected, professional circles can be small and highly interconnected. Someone at the institution you are interviewing with may very well know someone at your home institution. If they hear that you are a candidate—perhaps by seeing your name on a document or hearing you mentioned in conversation—they may reach out to their connection at your home institution to learn more about you. And you might wonder how they would find out. Because your candidacy can become public in so many ways that you cannot predict or prevent, you can do what I tell clients to do: "Ask for confidentiality and assume that it will not happen." Breaches of confidentiality happen, no matter how many promises are made. It's up to you to manage your message, and it's easier to manage if you plan for the surprises. Simply determine the ideal time to tell your boss and have an answer handy for anyone else who might hear of your candidacy and ask you about it.

CHAPTER 9 TOOL

Purpose and instructions

This list of common interview questions will help you prepare for the interview portion of your search process. Review them, and practice your responses with a trusted person who will give you good feedback.

Common interview questions you may be asked:
1. Tell me a little about yourself.
2. Why are you interested in this role or position?
3. What makes this position a good fit for you?
4. How has your career to date prepared you for this position?
5. What makes our organization a good fit for you?
6. What are your career goals in the short, medium and long term?
7. Could you explain this gap in your employment history?
8. What accomplishment are you most proud of?
9. Tell me about what you learned from the accomplishment you are most proud of.
10. Tell me about a failure you experienced and what you learned from it.
11. Why are you leaving your current position?
12. What do you consider the greatest successes of our organization?
13. What do you consider the greatest challenges of our organization?
14. What is your vision for this role or position?
15. What are your salary expectations?
16. Tell me about a difficult or bad boss you have experienced.
17. Describe a difficult employee situation you handled involving someone you supervised, and what you did to address the situation.
18. What is your greatest strength and how will it help you succeed in this role?
19. What is your greatest challenge and how will you overcome it in this role?
20. What skills or experience do you offer that will help you succeed in this role?
21. What is your understanding of the importance of diversity, inclusion, and belonging in the workplace?
22. How have you sought to maximize diversity, inclusion, and belonging in your leadership roles to date?
23. What is your leadership style?
24. What is the largest budget you have managed?
25. Why should we hire you?

And don't forget to prepare at least five questions you want to ask the interviewers – you may not get to ask them all, but have them available if you need them, and tailor your question to the context of the interview. Here are some sample questions YOU could (and perhaps should) ask:
1. What are the top two or three things the person selected for this position will need to address quickly?
2. What are the measures of success for the person selected for this position during the first year?
3. Are there key partnerships or collaborations that need to be built, maintained, or strengthened by the person selected for this position?
4. What are the top two or three opportunities for organizational growth that the person selected for this position should attend to?
5. Who are the key constituents whose viewpoints should be taken into consideration by the person selected for this position?

CHAPTER 9 – SUMMARY

This chapter provides an overview of the complex process of going through a job search from the application process up to the point where you receive an offer. It is a complex and busy time, particularly if you are active in more than one search at the same time. Managing your process and Very Next Action steps for each search, then planning for the interviews and your messaging strategy along the way are critical steps in this stage of the Career Transitions Cycle.

Core Concepts

- Maintain a working list of information about each search that you enter, so you can always know at a glance what the Very Next Action is for that search.

- Decide whether you should use a curriculum vitae or a résumé to tell your story in detail, and then update and tailor it to each position you are considering.

- Use your cover letter to describe the narrative arc of your career and clarify why you are excited to consider this opportunity and why you are a great fit for the role. Be sure to convey enthusiasm.

- Understand who will be making the hiring decision and be ready to work with the search consultant, the search committee, and others to share information and ask questions as needed.

- Prepare for the interview by planning answers to common questions.

- Use the PARL (Problem/Project, Action, Result, Learning) format to prepare two to three success stories and two to three stories of challenges to discuss if you are asked.

- Make a plan for communicating about your participation in the search and know that in most circumstances your boss should be the first to be informed, preferably by you directly.

- Ask for confidentiality from the search firm and committee, but assume it may not happen.

Key Takeaways

What are your Key Takeaways from this chapter? What did you learn, in your own words?

Very Next Actions

After reading this chapter, are there any Very Next Actions (VNAs) you need to take based on what you have learned?

VNA #1:

VNA #2:

Career Transition Stage 4 – Negotiation

At this point, you have received at least one offer for a new position, either in your existing organization or in a new one. You are wondering what to ask for and how to structure the negotiation. What is reasonable to request, can you ask for more, and what things are so important that you would reject the offer if you don't get them? This can be a tricky time that may lead you to question your value in the marketplace. You may be wondering if you should lowball your ask just to get the job, while those around you could be encouraging you to "ask for the moon" because "you won't get anything once the honeymoon is over."

Are these beliefs true? Are they consistent with your experience of the search? How do you know when you have gotten "enough?" Clients who are at this stage can be overwhelmed by concern and by advice from those around them, but they often also wonder if they should consult with an attorney or a financial planner, or both. Negotiation is also of particular interest to key stakeholders such as family members, and in some cases, people find themselves negotiating for more than one position at once. Finally, when negotiations near completion, people start asking themselves when to resign and how much notice they need to provide. These issues and many more will play themselves out as you successfully navigate the negotiation stage. Let's walk through what you need to know now.

Planning for Your Negotiation

Some helpful background on negotiation

If you are not a professional negotiator or have not been formally trained in negotiation, you will likely assume that you are negotiating in a "zero-sum" game, where you and the other party are competing to give or take from a finite pool of resources. This is considered a **distributed** negotiation, and it is characterized by an assumption that your negotiation is a competition, where resources are finite, someone must win, and someone must lose. Participants in this type of negotiation are typically motivated by self-interest and individual gain. The strategy in this approach is to negotiate a single issue (like salary) before negotiating other issues. Maintaining the integrity of personal and professional relationships between the negotiating parties is not a very high priority in the process.

An alternative approach is typically called **integrative** negotiation. This approach assumes resources are not fixed (this does not mean they are infinite, but they can be flexible), that all parties can navigate to a win-win (or win-win-win) solution that addresses their mutual interests and benefits all concerned. Discussions examine the issues in their totality, not one at a time, and the integrity of personal and professional relationships between the negotiating parties can be a very high priority.

Most job negotiations in the professional world have the potential to be integrative negotiations, though that is sometimes not possible. In general, I encourage people to take the integrative approach, if possible, because it assumes good intent, preserves relationships where possible, and generally is less adversarial. If it becomes clear that the other party is treating the negotiation as distributive, you may have to adjust, but it is helpful to begin this way, and plan for alternatives. Either way, it is important that you understand the approach you want to take, as it will determine your strategy, including how and when you ask for different items on your Working Negotiation List. For purposes of this discussion, I will assume you are pursuing an integrative negotiation strategy for the offer I hope is coming your way.

Know your negotiation partner(s)

When you enter any type of negotiation, it pays to know as much as you can about your negotiating partner. Who are they? What is their role? Will they make the final decision on the offer or will they need someone else to sign off on the agreement? If it's the latter, will you have a chance to talk to the final decision-maker? This is key information you need to understand *before* the negotiation begins. If you have been told an offer will be forthcoming or asked what would be important to you in an offer, it's perfectly acceptable to ask who you will be negotiating with and who holds the final approval authority for the offer or contract.

Once you know who you will be working with to reach an offer, it is important to try to understand what matters most to them. Although your negotiating partner may not have walked through the same formal process you have as you have read in this book, she will have a sense of what is important to her and the organization, and it will inform her position. It's tempting to see the person you're negotiating with as an adversary, but that's usually not constructive. You both have the same goal—getting you to an offer you're happy with, so you will accept the position. Treat her as if you both have a common goal, and you are trying to figure out how to achieve as much of what each of you want as possible.

In considering what matters to your negotiating partner, for example, consider these scenarios. Perhaps the hiring institution has previously offered this position to two people, neither of whom accepted. That may mean your negotiating partner is under real pressure to fill the position this time. Alternatively, this may be a highly competitive position with many other qualified candidates who could be considered if your negotiation does not yield an offer you are willing to accept. Perhaps there are significant fiscal constraints that mean salary is not very negotiable. Perhaps the hiring institution is working to bring new skills (skills you possess) into the organization, or maybe this is a new role. You could even be negotiating with someone who wanted the position you are now being offered. Because any of these considerations could affect the outcome of your negotiations, it will be important to know as much as you can about them when you plan your strategy.

What Can I Ask For, and What Matters?

If you have not given this aspect of the process much thought when it starts, you may feel flummoxed. The range of possibilities in a negotiation is almost always broader than my clients can imagine, but we often start by going back to the fundamentals. I suggest reviewing your Top Ten List of what matters most to you from Chapter 1. Those priorities should guide your negotiation. If your list is not up-to-date, take a bit of time to refresh it before you start. Then use it to identify everything you can think of to ask for that would maximize the things that matter most to you. It may be helpful to remember that list of rewards we discussed way back in Chapter 2, as you begin to plan your list of things to consider.

Monetary Items You Can Ask For

Monetary asks focus on things that have a price tag, things that someone could write a check for. Sometimes, these are called "tangible" items, but I think the concept of "monetary" items is clearer to most people. They can include compensation (pay and benefits, which typically recur or are provided on an annual or recurring basis) or non-compensation (things that cost money but are not given on a recurring basis).

Examples of compensation items include salary, bonus or incentive payments, commissions, retirement contributions, vacation time and other paid leave, holidays, insurance policies, and similar items. When organizations make an offer that includes a figure called "total compensation," that usually includes the monetary value of all these items. If you focus just on salary, you may miss an opportunity to negotiate a more desirable deal that includes some of these other items. And don't forget, when organizations negotiate these things, they see them as costs for many years ahead, not just the annualized cost for one year. They are also things that affect you for many years ahead, and the long-term value of even small increases in some of these benefits can be significant. It's worth discussing benefit negotiations with your financial planner to understand the long-term implications for you.

Examples of non-compensation monetary items include a signing bonus, relocation expenses, an office, a parking space, computer equipment, laboratory space, a cell phone, professional development funds (including funds to pay a professional executive coach, which is becoming a very common negotiating ask for leaders and new employees), research bridge funding (if you are in academia), a marketing budget (if you are in product development), staff support, a research assistant, and similar support items. These things may be one-time expenses or ongoing commitments. Be sure you are clear on what you are asking for and whether it is an ongoing budgetary need the institution will have to continue to fund, versus a one-time request. Bringing this understanding to the negotiation process will let the organization see that you understand finance and the implications to the organization, not just the implications for your bottom line.

The Intangibles That Can Tip the Balance

As you negotiate and determine whether you will take the position, don't forget the often-immutable factors that can make or break your happiness in a new role. If two offers are reasonably similar, they can help you make your final choice. If one offer is better than the other, they will help you put it in context. A generous salary and budget could pale in comparison to the happiness you will find on a small, beautiful campus with unlimited paid time off and freedom to be creative. It all comes back to what matters most to you. And then go into the specifics of things to think about that are listed here.

Non-monetary things typically don't have a price tag, and nobody needs to write a check for them. They are sometimes called "intangible" items, but again, I prefer the non-monetary label—it helps people think about them in a way that recognizes the costs to the organization, and this understanding can help you gain real value in your package without raising the overall price tag.

What do I mean by non-monetary items? Consider how much you like the environment—is the campus on which you work pleasant to drive to? Are there safe outdoor walking or exercise spaces nearby? Is remote work an option (or a necessity)? Is childcare provided? All these things are non-monetary things that may be important to you. Also, how will the relationships between you and colleagues or leadership develop? Will you be able to have a formal mentor assigned to you, or can you choose one? Is there a formal and structured mentoring program that assigns you someone who can guide your adaptation to the role and the organization? Do people seem to get along well? Does it feel like you would *want* to get up and go to work with these people every day? How did the organization handle the pandemic and post-pandemic planning for work life? Were they supportive of individuals' needs, or are they focused on the bottom line at all costs? How does the place feel in terms of stress, burnout, overwork (or the converse—calm, energized, and creative)? Is there an opportunity for you to advance beyond the position you are currently seeking? Will you be supported to develop along a path of advancement? How is the organization positioned within your industry? Is it a "brand name" organization, with national or international recognition? Or is it smaller, and does that lend it an opportunity to be nimbler and more creative?

Key Action Step – Make the List of Things You Want to Ask For

As you prepare for negotiation, it will be important to clarify what you care most about. I encourage people to make a clear list, and you should know that it's never too early in the Career Transitions Cycle to do this. It may inform the positions you pursue from the start, and it can always be updated as you gain more information about a particular position. Your list should include tangible and intangible, monetary (compensation and non-compensation) and non-monetary items. And, of course, it should be grounded in what matters most to you and your key personal stakeholders. Does your negotiation list of items line up with what you said in Chapter 1 was important? Has your Top Ten List of what matters most to you changed? What matters most in this negotiation? These are questions to ask yourself at every step in the search to offer and the negotiation phases.

Your Working Negotiation List

Once you have a sense of what you can and want to ask for, it's time to clarify your negotiation points. These go on your list of things you will ask for. I call it your Working Negotiation List, and it's your guide for discussions around negotiation. Once you have created your Working Negotiation List, review what's on that list, then divide the items into three categories:

- "Must-have" items—these are the things that, if you do not get them in the final offer, you will be willing to walk away. They are that important. Examples include a minimum salary, minimum levels of time off or opportunities for advancement. They can be monetary, non-monetary, compensation, or non-compensation. But they are critically important to your decision. Without them, you would be willing to walk away.

- "Nice-to-have" items—these are the things you really want, but if you don't get them, you could still negotiate to a satisfactory deal. You could use them to make some trade-offs, and you might end up with some of them but not others. In a word, they are negotiable, and you will use them to maximize your negotiation outcomes.

- "Pie-in-the-sky" items—I always urge clients to identify a couple of big or surprising asks. You might not get them, and maybe you can't even imagine them being considered. But the only way to know is to ask, and sometimes there are surprises. I've seen some clients and colleagues get some big-ticket and very positive enhancements to their offers this way. Always have one or two items like this on your negotiation list.

Reviewing the List

Once you have organized your Working Negotiation List into these three categories, ask yourself if there's anything you might have overlooked. It is possible you left off something you want but are afraid to ask for (probably because it belongs on your pie-in-the-sky list). It's also surprisingly easy to overlook a "must-have" that needs to be added. Remember your "nice-to-have" list provides some useful middle ground for making tradeoffs. Add anything that you have missed to the list.

Now, review your list with your key stakeholders (likely your spouse and a mentor or coach, maybe your children). Make one last pass to add or re-prioritize or change anything you still need to adjust or consider. This is your Working Negotiation List, and once it's done, you're ready to strategize for the negotiation.

Technical Negotiation Strategy

It will help your planning to have a little background on negotiation. These points will provide useful context:

- Negotiation is rarely a one-time conversation. It's a series of steps.

- Negotiation may begin in person, in writing, via video, or by email—recognize that you will need to be ready to adapt however the opening component presents itself and do your best to have a strategy to rely on, no matter how the negotiation begins.

- It's helpful to have a way of buying time to consider things or to close the current round of negotiation so you can regroup. I urge clients to have a way of doing so in their back pockets. You can say, "I need some time to consider this; when do you need my answer?" Or try, "I don't have enough information to make that decision today. The things I need to know include ..." Don't be rushed into a decision in the moment and in a meeting, unless you have already agreed that the decision will be made at or by that time.

- There is no perfect way to start putting terms on the table. The conversation may start with you, or the hiring institution may initiate negotiations. The important thing is to KNOW what you want and to have a plan for asking for it and responding to any answer you receive.

In addition to these concepts, there are some technical terms that will help you plan the strategy for your negotiation conversations.

BATNA

You may have heard the acronym BATNA[16] before. It stands for the "Best Alternative to a Negotiated Agreement." This is the action you will take if the negotiation cannot be settled satisfactorily. You might think of this as your "walkaway" strategy, but it's more than that. It's about all the choices before you if you are not able to reach an agreement on this position. For example, you could withdraw from the search and continue other searches, or start a new one. You could withdraw from the search and stay in your current job. You could storm out of the negotiations and end the relationship. Evaluate EVERY option of which you can think, then consider which is best for you. Hold that card in your pocket, and don't play it too soon. It's critical that YOU know what the BATNA is for you. This allows you to retain your own internal power over the negotiation, reminding yourself that there is, in fact, a point at which you would withdraw from the negotiation. If you forget that, you lose your power. If you remember it, you may not have to *exercise* that power, but you know that you can.

Reservation Price

Your reservation price is the lowest possible value of a deal that you would accept. Go back and look at the Must-Have items on your Working Negotiation List. That list should include only the things that, if you don't get them in the deal, you would exercise your BATNA and walk away from the negotiation. Go back and make sure you have that list the way you want it. *This portion of your list is your reservation price*. Don't let the word "price" in the negotiation fool you. Not everything in your reservation price is about money. Remember your monetary and non-monetary lists? The reservation price includes some intangible items, but you must have them. For example, suppose your daughter is a senior in high school.

---

[16] Fisher, Roger, and William Ury. 1981. *Getting to Yes: Negotiating Agreement Without Giving In*. London: Penguin Books.

You are given an offer in September, and she won't complete her final year of school until the following June. Allowing your daughter to finish high school without relocating might be on your list of must-haves, yet you now are faced with an offer that includes a January 1 start date. That means that you must either negotiate a later start date or be willing to live away from your spouse and daughter for a period of time. We'll come back to this scenario in a moment. The key point for now is that allowing your daughter to finish high school with her friends is a part of your reservation price.

Target Price

Your target price is the best possible outcome you could imagine. If you go back to your Working Negotiation List and add everything up, that is your target price. It's everything you want to ask for. You must ask for it if you want to get it. Returning to the scenario about your daughter, here's how that might play out. Let's say that your "nice to have" list includes you, your spouse, and your daughter all remaining together in your current location until your daughter finishes high school. You and your spouse do not have to live in separate locations, you get the new job you want, and you don't have to move until after she finishes school, so starting the new role after July 1 might be a pie-in-the-sky ask for you. That's your ideal scenario.

Your reservation price (your daughter finishing high school with her friends) does not change. What could change involves that "nice to have" list. While you and your spouse might agree to live apart for a period of time, you could negotiate a start date that keeps that period to a minimum. So, you might negotiate a March start date, for example, rather than a January start date you were initially offered. This is an example of using that "nice to have" list to negotiate a resolution that benefits you (and your stakeholders) as well as the other negotiating parties.

Let's talk for a moment about that pie-in-the-sky list—the things you think are so outrageous that nobody would ever give them to you, but you'd really love to have them. I suggest that everyone include at least one or two of these seemingly outrageous options in their initial ask for two reasons. First, if you don't ask, they will never know you wanted it, and so they are unlikely to give it (now or later). Second, it reinforces the idea that a negotiation is about asking for what you want and negotiating with the other parties to get to the best deal possible. So, ASK, already! Your pie-in-the-sky items are part of your target price.

Getting a pie-in-the-sky item is really exciting, but keep this part of your list in context. Getting something from this list should not have any effect on your must-haves or your nice-to-haves. Your must-have list is non-negotiable, your nice-to-have list can be used to "trade" for other things on the nice-to-have list, and your pie-in-the-sky list is the icing on top of the cake. So, if you get all the things on your nice-to-have and pie-in-the-sky lists but only some of the things on your must-have list, it's time to invoke your BATNA.

Your Negotiation Partner's BATNA, Reservation and Target Prices

Whether they formally know it or not (and many negotiators for professional jobs *do* know this), your negotiation partners have their own BATNA, reservation price, and target price. If you do not understand these concepts, they will figure that out quickly, and you will be at a disadvantage because they understand the process better than you do. Just know that they have these concepts in mind, and if you can strive to keep the dialogue constructive, rather than adversarial, you may gain a sense of what their BATNA, reservation, and targets could be, even if you don't have the details. You might think that the target price for the institution is simply the lowest monetary price tag they can get away with, and their reservation price is the maximum amount that they would give. Don't forget to consider the intangibles, the things that are driving the search, the uniqueness of what you bring to the position, and the current state of the labor market for this position. These things all may be more important than monetary items to the organization. Just giving yourself a bit of preparation time to consider their prices, and their BATNA, will strengthen the negotiation, even if their targets are very different than yours.

The Goal of Negotiation – the ZOPA

In most cases, a distributed negotiation that is conducted in good faith has as its goal not a win or a loss for either side, but rather the best deal possible, which is usually somewhere between the reservation and target prices for all parties involved. This is often termed the Zone of Possible Agreement, or ZOPA.[17] The more all parties know about what matters to the other parties, the more readily they can find a ZOPA that meets all parties' needs.

Executing Your Negotiation

At some point, you will be given an offer to consider. The terms give you a sense of the target price for your negotiation partner. It may not be final, but it's where they want to start. Review that offer, and think about how you want to counter—and YES, you should counter. The expectation is that this is a negotiation, not a "take it or leave it" kind of situation. This is your chance to ask for EVERYTHING that you might want, particularly all your must-have list, the nice-to-have list, and any pie-in-the-sky items. You don't identify which items are which to your negotiating partner, but you need to know where they are in your target price. By putting everything on the table, two things happen. All participants know pretty much what the target price is for the other parties, AND you don't land in the position of seeming to move the goalposts by later asking for things you left out of your initial counteroffer.

_____

[17] Watkins, Michael, and Susan Rosegrant. 2001. *Breakthrough International Negotiation: How Great Negotiators Transformed the World's Toughest Post-Cold War Conflicts.* San Francisco: Jossey-Bass.

Put your target price out there, and know privately what your reservation price is, and what your BATNA is if your reservation price is not met. Then start navigating through the ZOPA with a particular focus on your nice-to-have items as the items you can negotiate with. You can use them to enhance the terms of your offer, but you can also let go of them if they seem impossible or to increase your leverage for other things on your nice-to-have list, or perhaps even your pie-in-the-sky list. In essence, your nice-to-have list enables you to achieve the best possible negotiated agreement (the opposite of the BATNA). But it doesn't negate your must-have list, and your need to invoke the BATNA if you don't get your must-haves.

A Note About "Take-it-or-Leave-It" Offers

If you get a "take it or leave it" offer, you may want to seriously consider whether you want the position. If it does not meet your reservation price (your must-have list) and there is no room for negotiation, you may decide to exercise your best alternative (BATNA) and simply bow out of the process, as there is not really a process here anyway.

Addressing Bias in Negotiation

Much has rightly been written about the disparities in negotiation outcomes for men and women, and for people of color and other underrepresented minorities. Pay gaps exist between men and women, between college-educated black men and women and college-educated white men, between women of color and white women.[18] Pay disparities that affect people of color, LGBTQIA+ people, and other underrepresented groups are critically important to consider as you plan your negotiation. Even when applicants consistently ask for what they want, evidence suggests both implicit and

---

[18] Bleiweis, Robin, Jocelyn Frye, and Rose Khattar. "Women of Color and the Wage Gap." Center for American Progress, November 17, 2021. https://www.americanprogress.org/article/women-of-color-and-the-wage-gap/.

explicit race- and gender-based bias play a role in the negotiation process,[19] sometimes resulting in outcomes that are inequitable.

Much more needs to be studied, written, and changed about these issues. That work is beyond the scope of this book, but it is critical context for your negotiation, so it's worth discussing a few suggestions for managing your process if you think that bias might be at play. Things that may be helpful include:[20]

- Assess your own biases before you enter the negotiation. What assumptions are you making about those involved in the negotiation (including yourself)? How might these assumptions be tested? How might they help or hinder you in the process?

- Assess the biases of the others involved. What can you observe about their statements, behavior, and assumptions? If you experience an explicit example of bias, you might need to call it out, such as "why would you say that to me?" or "what is it about me that causes you to draw that conclusion/ask that question/make that assumption?"

- Give yourself time to process your own reaction to what has happened before you decide how to respond—slow things down to allow time to deal with your own experience of the situation.

---

[19] Staff, Program on Negotiation. "Counteracting Negotiation Biases Like Race and Gender in the Workplace." Daily Blog. Harvard Law School Program on Negotiation, May 9, 2023. https://www.pon.harvard.edu/daily/leadership-skills-daily/counteracting-racial-and-gender-bias-in-job-negotiations-nb/.

[20] Dickinson, Alexandra. "3 Strategies to Change Biases in a Negotiation." Forbes Leadership. August 17, 2017. https://www.forbes.com/sites/alexandradickinson/2017/08/17/3-strategies-to-change-implicit-biases-in-a-negotiation/?sh=7f3308472038.

- Do your homework and plan your negotiation ahead of time—it's easier to stand your ground, maintain your composure, and not get derailed if you have thought through a plan ahead of time.

- Consider what tools are available to you for finding benchmarks about salary in your industry and go find them, so you can set realistic reservation and target prices for your negotiation.

- Complete your Working Negotiation List and review it with key stakeholders.

- Know your negotiation partners and what is likely to drive them.

- Remember that asking for what you want and need to be successful in the role is a key leadership skill. Don't negotiate with yourself before you get in the room and lower your own perception of your value.

- Know what matters to you regarding diversity and inclusion. In fact, a welcoming and diverse environment that provides opportunity and encouragement to all on an equal or equitable footing may even be part of your "must have" list. If that's the case (it is for me), then pay close attention throughout the search process for signs you should trigger your BATNA.

Choosing a Team of Professional Advisors

I am a firm believer in the idea that we all need a team of professionals as we navigate our professional and personal lives, and this is never truer than in a contract negotiation. You should not go it alone at this juncture. You might think that the cost of hiring a professional to assist you is significant, but it is often much less than you think and far less in the long run than the cost of a negotiation or contract mistake. It may also enhance the outcome of your negotiation, yielding more value over time than the short-term investment in professional services.

At a minimum, I suggest that you consult with your financial advisor and your attorney to review your strategy, your needs, and your approach to this negotiation. I also recommend reviewing any contract or legal documents with an attorney. If you have a professional coach as part of your team for this process, remember that they are not able to provide legal or financial advice, unless they are also trained in those areas. Each member of your team has her or his own expertise, and it helps to be clear about what that is and how you will work with each of them. Once you have successfully completed your negotiation, it's a good idea to review the final agreement with your team before you sign the offer letter or the contract.

Once you have signed, CELEBRATE!!! Congratulations on a successful negotiation. You've earned this job and the terms you have achieved. And now you're ready for the next chapter and your next step in the Career Transitions Cycle—Offboarding and Onboarding.

CHAPTER 10 TOOL

Purpose of the exercise

This Working Negotiation List will help you plan your strategy for negotiating a new job offer (or really anything).

Instructions

Make a list of items you want and need to feel that you have had a successful negotiation.

- **"Must-have" items** — these are the things that, if you do not get them in the final offer, you will be willing to walk away. They are that important. Examples include a minimum salary, minimum levels of time off or opportunities for advancement. They can be monetary, non-monetary, compensation or non-compensation. But they are critically important to your decision.
- **"Nice-to-have" items** — these are the things you really want, but if you don't get them, you could still negotiate to a satisfactory deal. You could use them to make some tradeoffs, and you might end up with some of them but not others. In a word, they are negotiable, and you will use them to maximize your negotiation outcomes.
- **"Pie-in-the-sky" items** — I always urge clients to identify a couple of big or surprising asks. You might not get them, and maybe you can't even imagine them being considered. But the only way to know is to ask, and sometimes there are surprises. I've seen some clients and colleagues get some big-ticket and very positive enhancements to their offers this way. Always have one or two items like this on your negotiation list.

Must-Have Items	Nice-to-Have Items	Pie-in-the-Sky Items

CHAPTER 10 – SUMMARY

Negotiation is a process. Integrative, rather than distributive, negotiation strategies often yield the best agreements for all parties involved, but you'll need to understand some basic terminology and context to get the best agreement for you. Planning for your negotiation and implementing your plan systematically will help you avoid underselling yourself.

Core Concepts

- Planning for your negotiation is critical. Start by getting clear on what you want and need. Your list of What Matters Most to You from Chapter 1 can be a fantastic starting place for mapping this out.

- Consider both monetary and non-monetary items that you want or need in the final agreement.

- Your reservation price, or the lowest-value deal you are willing to accept, should include everything on your must-have list.

- Your target price, or the highest value deal you could negotiate, should include everything on your list. This becomes the foundation of your Working Negotiation List.

- Once you have made your initial list of asks on your Working Negotiation List, categorize them into must-haves, nice-to-haves, and pie-in-the-sky asks.

- Have a plan and a strategy that includes an understanding of the other parties in the negotiation, what matters to them, and their reservation and target prices.

- Understand your alternatives to a successful negotiation—your BATNA. This is your backup plan. Know when you would be willing or ready to implement it.

- Don't be afraid to ask for everything you want at the outset. It's a negotiation. Playing your cards close to the chest and dribbling out extra asks as you proceed is not a professional approach to negotiation and may make the other parties feel that you are moving the goalposts.

- Be aware that implicit and explicit bias can affect negotiations and may affect yours. If an inclusive environment is on your list of must-haves, you should be especially attuned to this issue.

- Enlist a team of professionals to assist you. At a minimum, consider including your financial planner and your attorney. You may want to work with a professional coach as well. Each of these team members will have different roles to play. Consult them early and develop a clear plan for how each of them will support you through the negotiation process.

Key Takeaways

What are your Key Takeaways from this chapter? What did you learn, in your own words?

Very Next Actions

After reading this chapter, are there any Very Next Actions (VNAs) you need to take based on what you have learned?

VNA #1:

VNA #2:

Career Transition Stage 5 – Offboarding and Onboarding

Once you have accepted a position and notified both your new employer and your current leadership that you are making a transition, you are officially in the Onboarding and Offboarding Stage. These two sets of work (onboarding and offboarding) usually happen simultaneously as you leave one role and move to another, perhaps in another organization. Whom do you tell first? And who should be next in line? How do you manage the message of your transition effectively? You may wonder how others will talk about your transition, whether you can manage their narrative and what that narrative would ideally be. This is always tricky, and especially if you are leaving because something difficult has happened in your current role. If that's the case, should you leave telling people all about it, or do you keep the story to yourself? Do you leave gracefully or not-so-gracefully?

Surely, you are also thinking about the tasks you need to wrap up and how to prepare for the person who will come behind you. Do you want or need to influence anything about the selection of your successor? Do you have any ability or power to do so? And how do you handle the grief of leaving? Even though it's your choice, you probably will experience some complicated emotions.

You're probably also thinking a lot about your new role. Should you start attending meetings and doing other things, even though you haven't officially started? What if the new organization asks you to do so—will they understand that you still have obligations at your current job? You are probably also thinking of logistics, things like moving your office, your home, and your basic life necessities).

These examples are just a few of the thoughts and questions that come up in this stage. It's an intense period that can be both exhilarating and exhausting. While there's a lot going on at this time, I've found four key themes that seem to create the most stress during this stage. They are:

- communication about the transition
- managing the tasks of onboarding
- managing the tasks of offboarding
- managing your time and energy while doing all of this

Let's dive in and see how to help you thrive through it all.

Communication about Your Transition

Creating an Intentional Communication Strategy

Communication about your transition began at the point that you told anyone you were in a search process. That may have been several stages ago, or you may just be starting. Either way, by this time, your current boss and your new one likely both know what is underway. But if you haven't, you'll need to tell your team as well as any others who work closely with you on projects or whose work and advancement depend upon you in some fashion. There may be others who will be less directly affected by your transition, though they may still have a stake in it. Then there are the folks who are simply curious about what is going on. Managing communication with each of these groups takes some work, and the more planning you have done about communication strategies before committing to a job, the better you will be able to manage surprises or challenges that come up. Invest the time as early in your transition process as you can to plan your communication strategy.

To structure this process, I suggest that you think about a series of concentric circles containing all the people who need information about your transition. The circles are made up of people who have differing proximity to you and differing "need to know" levels about what is going on. Some of these groups will be defined by your work together, and some will be defined more by their importance in terms of personal or professional relationships, rather than operational details.

I think of the smallest group among your concentric circles as Zone 1, people with whom you collaborate most closely and those who report directly to you. They have the most acute need to know what you are planning and the timeline and the succession plan for each of your projects. They will also want to know anything you can share about the person taking over your role. Develop a list of the projects and people who fall into Zone 1, make sure to plan for each of those projects, and then begin to tell the people. No matter how well you plan for the handoff of your projects, once you have relinquished your role, you also relinquish control over related personnel assignments and even whether the project continues. Planning for communicating with these people clearly and early will enable you to set minds at ease.

Sometimes this information can be conveyed in one large group meeting, but more often, it is best done in a series of private or small-group conversations. If you go with smaller settings, know that the sequence of these conversations is sometimes important. You need to plan for who should be told first and who can find out a bit later; you also need to plan for handling things if anyone shares your news before you are ready, upsetting your strategy. Finally, you need to plan for how to talk with people whose career progress may be affected by your decisions. In this latter situation, reassuring them in a private conversation that you will continue to advocate for them (if that is your intent) can go a long way. All Zone 1 communications are typically best done face to face, and not via email.

After you have a plan for Zone 1, think about the next "ring" of people around you. The people in Zone 2 are those whose primary concern is logistics, such as signatory authority or purchasing decisions during the transition, and whose work is directly impacted by your transition. Those in Zone 2 will want to know your timeline and who will take over those tasks after your departure. You may benefit from their help as you work through these considerations since they may think of things you have not.

Zone 2 might include support staff, business managers for specific projects or initiatives, human resources professionals, peers, and colleagues. Some of these conversations may need to occur in person or by videoconference, but some may be appropriate in just a brief and clear email. The information needed here is often technical and operational. Communication may still benefit from staging so that one group knows before others, but it's less critical to do so for Zone 2 than in Zone 1.

Zone 3 people are those who are not directly affected by your work transition, but who care about you personally or professionally. They may be friends, peers, colleagues, or mentors. Although they have not fallen into Zones 1 and 2, you may still want to invest time in a personal conversation that is appropriate to your relationship. These are often private discussions, and they often focus on relationships and the future of those relationships. They may include gratitude for the way these people have affected your career or for their help in your growth and readiness for this new opportunity. I think of this as the "friends and work family" zone. Tailor your conversations to each relationship and devote some energy to managing them well. You will typically be very glad you did, as you can cement lifetime friendships that transcend organizational and role-related boundaries. It's worth the time it will take to have these conversations intentionally.

Zone 4 is what I think of as the public group. It includes people who are curious about what you are doing but are not personally or professionally affected by your transition. Typically, reaching Zone 4 means you've reached the point in your communication strategy where you send out an email to the entire organization announcing your change. Sometimes your current boss will want to send that note, but it's OK if you ask for the chance to contribute to the wording and the timing of the message. I also recommend that you not reach out to Zone 4 until you have completed the communication with Zones 1-3. Sometimes others make that impossible. I have seen supervisors pre-empt a communication plan by sending a note to the organization before the person leaving the role is ready. If that happens to you, know that having plans in place for Zones 1-3 will help you act quickly. That's why I recommend thinking through your whole plan before you get too far into the communication process.

Managing the Narrative of Your Transition

Sometimes, my clients get upset when they hear others mention rumors about their transition plans. They are surprised by how quickly they enter the "lame duck" state, where they feel they don't have information or decisional authority even though they are still in the role. My advice here is to remember that you cannot control what others decide to say. But you CAN craft a clear and positive message and then work diligently to put it forward. It starts with developing the clear and intentional communication strategy as we described above. The narrative itself—the words you will use to tell the story of your transition—is just as important as the strategy. My clients often find it helpful to hear what works for others, so I've listed some key messages that I have helped clients craft in the bullets below. Take the ones you like, modifying them as needed, and create your own if that feels more appropriate to you. These are just examples of what you might choose to say.

- I've been offered a fantastic opportunity to grow, and while I will miss working with you, I am so grateful for getting to work with you. You have been instrumental in my success.

- I'm going to a great opportunity, but there is nothing here that pushed me to go. The opportunity is such a great one that I'm drawn toward it.

- I wasn't looking because I was dissatisfied. This is simply the natural progression of my professional work and career, and I'm excited about the chance to take on a new role.

- Thank you for sharing what you said about my contributions being critical here. You will be fine as I move forward, and here's what I know about the plan for after my transition. You have my full support and confidence. You are ready to step forward into new things as I move on.

These comments can be tailored to your situation. People may say things like, "We won't be able to succeed if you go," or, "I don't know what we will do without you." These sentiments are perhaps flattering, but generally people who are saying them need reassurance more than they need to have you respond to anything specific they have said. It's appropriate and kind to offer enough information to reasonably help them manage their anxiety about the potential change, and you don't have to share a lot of detail to accomplish this. Pay attention to what is worrying them and provide whatever reassurance you feel is reasonable.

Sometimes people will say or ask something that you are not prepared to share. You don't have to discuss anything you're not ready for. It's fine to simply say, "I'm not able to discuss that part of the transition," or "I don't have an answer about what our organization/group/team will do about that, but I know that others are working on it."

Remember, managing your message is generally served best if you stay positive, reassure where you can, and don't make promises you won't be able to keep. Don't worry about becoming a lame duck if that happens. As we explore the offboarding and onboarding tasks before you, you may see a reduction in decisional or informational authority as a relief during this period.

The Tasks of Offboarding

The tasks of offboarding depend heavily on the role and institution, but there are some patterns that predictably apply to most professionals. Some things you can expect to attend to at this time include:

- ✓ Taking inventory of all the projects for which you have any responsibility and developing a strategy for handing them off or shutting them down.

- ✓ Reviewing all the standing committees and meetings you attend or lead and beginning to hand off your responsibilities in a professional way. You may or may not have influence over who takes your place, but it's important to assess which you want to try to influence and develop a plan for it.

- ✓ Completing your own committed work for your current organization. You may have reports, manuscripts, or projects to bring to completion before you leave. Make a calendar that maps out deadlines, and if deadlines don't exist, build them in for yourself.

- ✓ Developing and managing your communication strategy for Zones 1-4 and crafting the narrative you will tell others.

- ✓ Making time for all that communication with people in Zones 1-4. These conversations take time and must be scheduled in many instances.

✓ Cleaning out your office. This may include giving away, donating, or gifting some things, and deciding what can and should be discarded rather than moved with you.

✓ Resigning from professional commitments that are organization-dependent (an example from my coaching practice includes helping physicians remember to end their hospital privileges and supervisory duties over others in their practice).

✓ Talking to your human resources department about the transition of your benefits. I can't overemphasize this one. Make sure you understand what happens and what tasks you need to complete to maintain or transition things like health and other insurance policies, retirement plans and contributions, faculty appointments or other memberships related to your job, and many other things. Your HR professional will be able to help you with this and may already have a detailed checklist you can use.

✓ Talk with your personal financial and legal advisors about how your transition will affect your personal affairs.

✓ If you are moving, prepare your current home for sale and/or moving.

✓ This last one may be the most important consideration. Stay in close and clear contact with your personal stakeholders about what they are managing for you and the family. This may include a spouse or partner, your older children, and others in your household. They are going through their own transition, and making time to communicate with them regularly, clearly, and compassionately is critical in this stage.

The Tasks of Onboarding

While the tasks of onboarding also vary with the specifics of the new setting, some things are common and predictable. Consider these items in your planning:

- ✓ Have a conversation with your new boss/supervisor about expectations for what you will be doing during the transition stage. Be clear about your responsibilities and what you are technically authorized to do. Ask your new boss or an HR professional to help you plan the onboarding process during this time.

  - Your new boss is likely to want you to be reading and learning and may send over a lot of information for you to study. This is not unreasonable but must be prioritized during this very busy time.

  - Your new organization may urge you to attend meetings and even make decisions related to your new role. If this happens, consider designating someone there as your deputy, and develop a relationship with them so that they make decisions and inform you appropriately. DO NOT agree to make decisions yourself before you are legally authorized to do so. In most cases, if you are not employed by the organization, you can't make decisions.

- ✓ Your new team will want to know more about you. Planning some virtual coffee meetings with small groups to get acquainted is reasonable during this time, but you won't have a lot of space in your calendar. I have often suggested a monthly informal videoconference, tailored to different groups of staff and other personnel. To determine whom you should connect with, think about the people in Zones 1-4 that we discussed earlier. Those zones exist at the new organization, too, and you can plan your communication there using the same strategy.

✓ Remember that people at your new organization need reassurance too. They don't know what you will want to change, how you will behave, how you make decisions or even how you like to communicate. They are probably nervous. Give them enough time to begin getting to know you. Talk to your leadership about how to do this and whether there are any specific items that need to be addressed before you officially start.

✓ Attend to professional details such as credentialing, licensure, privileges, memberships, and similar issues, so that you are professionally ready to go when you arrive.

✓ Review committee assignments that you will be expected to take on and educate yourself about the membership and role of those committees.

✓ Talk with anyone critical to help you migrate projects such as ongoing research, benchmark reports that come due during your transition, and other ongoing key deliverables from your current organization to your new one, if applicable.

✓ Discuss your new benefits package with your onboarding organization—how and when will health insurance coverage begin? Are there specific items you need to address for you or your family? Will you need COBRA coverage during the transition? What do you need to do to roll over retirement funds into a new plan, or will you not want to do that? Your financial planner should be helpful here as well.

✓ Ask for a recommendation for a real estate agent if you have not already selected one. Give yourself time to make a decision about your new home if that's part of your transition. Understand that you may need to rent for several months before making a final decision about a home purchase.

✓ If you are moving to a new community, make a list of key services you will want to have in place when (or before) you arrive. These could include hairdresser, dry cleaner, grocery store, and health care providers, for example. Ask your professional advisors such as your financial planner and attorney if they can continue to work with you, or if they can make recommendations about new team members in your new area.

✓ As with the offboarding process, don't forget to include your key personal stakeholders in this process—ask them what they want to do, know, and learn about during this transition. Involve them in discussions about how the transition is going.

Managing Your Time and Energy MATTERS

As you can see from the lists above (which are incomplete, by the way), this is a very busy time. It can be overwhelming, so you will also want to be sure to keep the pace reasonable and take care of yourself. Some key tips for managing your own time and energy during this time include:

✓ Don't forget to rest and exercise during this time.

✓ Talk to your personal stakeholders, particularly a spouse or partner if you have one, to coordinate which things each of you will do. Know that you may become frustrated with one other, or excited about the prospects for your life together—often at different times. Make room for the dance of emotions between you. This process will happen for you with your children as well.

✓ You cannot possibly do everything you imagine needs to be done, and some things will simply *not* get done. The closer you get to your transition, the more you may understand this. Know that it's OK. Do the best you can and make a habit of taking things off your list every week by delegating to others or just deciding they won't get done.

✓ Take time to map out your timeline for this transition. Create a schedule for your checklist and try to be realistic. Do this at the outset of this stage, then modify it every week. Things will change. The importance of items on the list will change. That's OK.

✓ Know that other people in your life may be anxious, scared, angry or happy. It is not possible for you to manage all their emotions. Craft a simple response that you can use when others are struggling, such as, "I know this is hard, but it's all going to work out. We just have to get through it." This applies at home and at work.

✓ Be kind and gentle to yourself and those around you.

✓ Don't forget to rest and exercise. And REST some more.

CHAPTER 11 TOOL

Purpose of the exercise

This tool will help you plan for communication about an upcoming job change, strategizing who needs to know what is happening from you, and in what sequence.

Instructions

Use the diagram below to create a list of people with whom you will need to communicate about your transition. Use this list to plan the content, timing, and sequencing of your communication strategy. The table below will help you organize the list.

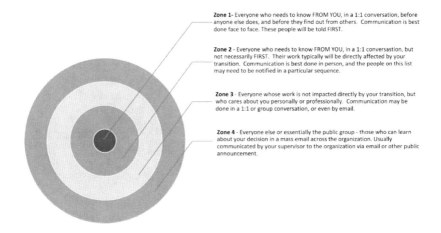

Zone 1- Everyone who needs to know FROM YOU, in a 1:1 conversation, before anyone else does, and before they find out from others. Communication is best done face to face. These people will be told FIRST.

Zone 2 - Everyone who needs to know FROM YOU, in a 1:1 conversastion, but not necessarily FIRST. Their work typically will be directly affected by your transition. Communication is best done in person, and the people on this list may need to be notified in a particular sequence.

Zone 3 - Everyone whose work is not impacted directly by your transition, but who cares about you personally or professionally. Communication may be done in a 1:1 or group conversation, or even by email.

Zone 4 - Everyone else or essentially the public group - those who can learn about your decision in a mass email across the organization. Usually communicated by your supervisor to the organization via email or other public announcement.

Zones of Communication
Page 2

Zones	Key Elements of Message	Timing and Sequence of Communication	Date Communication Planned	Communication Completed
Zone 1				
Zone 2				
Zone 3				
Zone 4				

NOTES:

CHAPTER 11 – SUMMARY

The transition stage of offboarding and onboarding is a very busy time. Planning your communication strategies and having a manageable task list during this time can be very helpful. This work takes time and energy. Core challenges for you during this stage will be the management of your own time and energy, understanding the tasks that need to be completed, and clear communication wherever possible. It is also important to recognize that others will have their own personal and professional responses to the transition that you cannot always mitigate or make better.

Core Concepts

- Communicating strategically can ease your transition, and planning ahead helps avoid surprises.

- You can't always manage the narrative other people tell, but you can keep your own narrative consistent. In many cases, people will notice and adopt your narrative themselves.

- Key offboarding tasks, if done well, can help maintain good relationships with the organization you are exiting. However, you cannot protect everyone from the impact of your exit.

- Key onboarding tasks are critical to your first impressions in the new organization or role. You will likely be asked or tempted to start those tasks early. Set good boundaries to avoid taking on responsibilities that are inappropriate during the transition and to build healthy relationships for the future.

- During this phase, there is a lot of real work to be done, both in your current and future role, and in managing relationships at home and professionally. You cannot manage everything without a plan, and you cannot protect everyone from the transition. But you MUST protect your own time and energy.

Key Takeaways

What are your Key Takeaways from this chapter? What did you learn, in your own words?

Very Next Actions

After reading this chapter, are there any Very Next Actions (VNAs) you need to take based on what you have learned?

VNA #1:

VNA #2:

Career Transition Stage 6 –
Setting Yourself Up for Success

In this stage, you have managed the onboarding and offboarding process, though there may still be some loose ends to tie up. Your attention is likely shifting to the impression you want to make in your new role, and the people you need to build relationships with as you begin. Who will want to talk with you, and who will need to hear from you?

It is a busy time. How do you manage your calendar and time as you start and for the first ninety days? How do you manage to stay excited when this whole process has been stressful and tiring?

You are probably also wondering about the measures of success that matter to you and to your organization. Are those metrics clear and achievable? Can they be negotiated or revisited if they are not working? Do you have the physical and operational tools you need to do your job (equipment, space, support staff, and even mundane things like a parking space and a map of the facility)?

These are questions people often ask during the opening phase of a new role. This is a critical stage because you only get that one proverbial chance to make a first impression, and you want to get it right. The goal here is to start off well and land back at Stage A, where you are once again happy and thriving in a job you enjoy, where you are building new skills and relationships.

Culture, People, and Resources

Congratulations! You've arrived at last in the new role you've worked so hard to achieve. You have a lot to learn about the organization (and even if you don't think you do, don't make the mistake of telling people you don't have anything to learn). As with every other stage of the Career Transitions Cycle, taking an intentional and thoughtful approach to this period truly does set you up for near-term and long-term success.

Learning your way around requires learning the organization and its culture, learning the process by which it operates, getting to know the people, and understanding the resources available to you and the mechanisms for obtaining those resources. This chapter is devoted to helping you create a plan for all of this. The whole process could take you as long as two to three years, and you should realize that your learning will never end. You will eventually have the basics down, but the organization and everything around it will continually evolve—and so will you. That's why the process I outline here is useful at any stage of the Career Transitions Cycle, although it's particularly helpful as you start your new role.

Learning the Organization and its Culture

Walking through the door on your first day can be disorienting. This is not because you're still learning where the restrooms are and how to get a cup of coffee. You need to really learn the organization and its culture. I don't just mean the mission, vision, and values of the organization as they are written on plaques or posters around the buildings, though those are important documents to review. I mean understanding who holds formal and informal power and decisional authority, how the organization has historically worked to achieve its goals, how the institution is oriented within the professional discipline and its own community. I mean how the organization prioritizes its goals and obligations, and how it communicates about them.

The most important skill you can develop to learn and integrate this information is to be a studious observer of human behavior. If you are someone who likes to keep a journal, I encourage you to start a new journal about your leadership journey in this organization. If you are not a journal-keeper, make time at least weekly, but potentially at the end of each workday, to take note of the things you are observing. What's important is being intentional about reviewing what you are learning about the culture. Who is making various types of decisions? Who is sharing information? Who is treating others well and with respect, and who might not be? One question I suggest clients to ask themselves in a new organization is, "Who are the 'wisdom-keepers'?" Wisdom-keepers may not hold formal power or authority, but they know and truly understand what is going on. In my own career, I have found wisdom-keepers among the building services or janitorial staff, security staff, administrative support staff, frontline contributors to the mission, middle-management, and sometimes even among senior leadership. It's important to figure out who understands the heart of the organization, so you can ask for their support. I advise clients to ask wisdom-keepers what they think you should know about the organization as you settle in.

This process will take time, and it will sometimes look like trying to map out a chess board in three time zones. Take note, however, that it is worthwhile. Sometimes clients will tell me that they don't have time for "all this political stuff." My response, particularly if they are in a leadership role, is, "You don't have time to **not** do it." This kind of information can make or break your success, and it is at the heart of the leadership mindset that will set you and your work apart.

Connecting with People

How do you get to know the people in a new (and potentially large) organization? Remember the concentric circles (Zones 1-4) we discussed in the chapter on offboarding and onboarding? A similar approach can be useful for getting acquainted with the people in your new organization. Here's how I adapt this model for the Setting up for Success stage. Think about who belongs in Zone 1 of your new institution. This group probably includes your direct boss and her or his boss. Zone 1 probably also includes your administrative assistant, if you have one, and the people who will be reporting directly to you. These people can tell you what is expected of you, what they need to know from you to do their jobs and how they like to share information. This may be a relatively small- to medium-sized group. It will be important that you meet with them and get to know them quickly, hopefully within the first few weeks.

In Zone 2, you will find collaborators, colleagues, peers, community stakeholders, and others. These people are critical to your long-term success, but they do not give or receive direction to you or from you. You can take a bit more time to get to know this group, but it will be important that you communicate to them early that you'd like to meet, that they are important to your learning, and that you value their input.

Zone 3 is likely to include people you want to develop relationships with as organizational mentors, outside stakeholders, and key senior leadership. It might seem counterintuitive to group these people all together because you will have different reasons for meeting with them, different goals and approaches for those meetings, and varying degrees of access to them. What is common among them is that they will take time to identify, and it will take time to foster these connections. Zone 3 is not less important than Zones 1 and 2, just less clearly visible when you first start in a new organization. What is important is that you begin building your list of people in Zone 3 early (potentially even before you arrive and begin your new role), and that you understand that it may take you months, or even more than a year, to identify and meet with them all, and it may take even longer to build working professional relationships with them. Plan early and execute this part of your strategy over time.

Identifying Available Resources

When I was an academic department chair, I used to say that I had access to five key resources:

1. People and their designated working time

2. Money or budgetary resources

3. Space for offices, labs, or other work

4. Equipment

5. Goodwill

I also recognized that I could lose any of those resources at a moment's notice, and goodwill was the only resource I could craft *de novo*. Because goodwill is dependent on building and nurturing relationships over time, I learned that I could leverage it to influence the availability or trajectory of the other resources. That's part of why the Setting Up for Success stage is so heavily focused on relationships. This doesn't mitigate the importance of other work, such as developing the ability to make decisions quickly. It simply underscores that relationships are an extremely valuable tool in your toolkit, and they are worth cultivating.

Even if you don't adopt my approach to resources, I encourage you to take stock of what you do have at your disposal. Once you understand the resources on your list, take time to learn how to acquire resources—this is critical to your success. Even if you are not a leader, there will be resources you need to acquire. Understanding how to do that within the organizational culture and processes will help you be successful. Ask about the budget process and when it happens. Also ask who manages the budget for your unit, and if it's you, try to understand how you can contribute to the development of that budget and its inputs and outputs. Ask yourself about intangible resources that may not have a price tag associated, though they are critical in your work environment. Go back to your list of non-monetary compensation that you developed in your negotiation process. How does that list apply now that you have the job? What resources from that list do you have at your disposal, and can you use them to incentivize those around you?

It has been said that leadership is the ability to command resources in the service of a vision that you get to set. Key to successfully implementing your vision is understanding how to leverage the resources at your disposal and how to obtain those that are not, so that you can achieve your own vision, one step at a time.

Crafting, Communicating, and Implementing Your Vision

Let's talk for a moment about your vision for your new role. You were likely asked in your interview to describe that vision, and you will be pressed to share the details of your vision for others to see as you come onboard. What should this process look like? Your vision will be informed by what you learn about the culture, processes, people, and resources of the organization around you. It should be a dynamic and evolving set of ideas that are not cast in stone at least until you have talked with people in Zones 1 and 2, and until you understand something about the culture of decision-making and processes for obtaining resources. Typically, it can take six to nine months before your vision solidifies into anything resembling an actionable plan. Let it evolve and tell people it's evolving. Even if you have a clear vision, if you make the mistake of sticking to the first version of your vision, rather than letting it shift as you learn, you will be seen as rigid and perhaps as unwilling to adapt. These perceptions will not help you succeed.

Communicating about your vision is an important part of managing those perceptions. Tell people that you crafted a vision that will be informed by what you learn as you settle into the organization. Let them know that as your vision evolves, you welcome their input and feedback.

Remind them (and yourself) that implementation of your vision will take time—and it will likely evolve throughout your tenure in your new role. It's not a one-and-done kind of thing, not remotely.

Techniques to Stage Your Onboarding

As you settle into your onboarding, I want to share two techniques that are useful at this step: Key Informant Interviews and the Snowball Technique.

Key Informant Interviews

The name of this technique is somewhat self-explanatory, and it's not difficult to understand. The idea is that you figure out who your "Key Informants" are as you get yourself onboarded, and then plan for a conversation with those people. I typically suggest that you develop a handful of interview questions, then ask the same questions of all Key Informants who are at a given level in the organization. This means a list for those above you, a list for those who will be reporting to you, and a list for those who are peers or colleagues. As you will see in the suggestions below, the lists can be somewhat similar, just modified to account for the level at which the informant works. Here are some sample questions for each group:

For Those Above You in the Organization (those you report to and those they report to):

- What are the most important things that someone in my position should know about the organization and about my unit?

- What are the top three opportunities the organization and my unit should be looking at on the horizon?

- What are the top three things you want me to be focusing on for the next ninety days? The next year?

- How will you know and measure whether I have been successful in my new role?

- How do you like to receive information? Format (email, text, phone call), level of detail (bullet points, paragraphs, other), and frequency? What are key things I should *always* bring to you? What are key things I should *not* bring to you?

- Who are the wisdom-keepers in the organization—those who know how things really operate, even if they are not in obvious positions of power or authority?

- Who else should I be talking with?

For Those Who Will Report to You (staff, team members, anyone you will be formally evaluating):

- Tell me about your job as you understand it.

- Do you have the tools and resources you need to do your job well?

- What are your primary career goals?

- What is most important to you that I pay attention to in the next ninety days? The next year?

- How will you know and measure whether I have been successful in my new role?

- Who are the wisdom-keepers in the organization—those who know how things really operate, even if they are not in obvious positions of power or authority?

- Who else should I be talking with?

For Peers, Colleagues, and Others You Want to Listen to or Gather Input From:

- What are the most important things you think someone in my position should be aware of about the organization and my unit?

- What are the top three things I should focus on for the next ninety days? The next year?

- What key partnerships should I be exploring?

- How will you know and measure whether I have been successful in my new role?

- How will I know if you think I should be doing something differently?

- Who are the wisdom-keepers in the organization—those who know how things really operate, even if they are not in obvious positions of power or authority?

- Who else should I be talking with?

These questions are not meant to be all-inclusive, and you should feel free to mix and match among my sample questions as you see fit. Choose three to five questions, and for each interview meeting, ask the same questions of everyone on a given level. Then, let them talk about whatever else they want to share with you. You'll get some consistent information on important questions, but their unscripted answers will be informative. Also, be sensitive to the concerns of those who will report to you. Sharing your questions ahead of time with them may help alleviate some anxiety about "meeting with the boss." Be sure to tell them you're just seeking to learn and that you are happy to hear about things beyond that list; it's just a starting point for conversation.

The Snowball Technique

Did you notice that each list above ended with the same two questions? "Who are the wisdom-keepers?" and "Who else should I be talking with?" These questions can help launch a useful process known as the Snowball Technique. This technique provides a means of ensuring you connect with everyone (and not just the obvious people) who can teach you about culture, processes, people, and resources in the organization. As you ask these questions and connect with more people, your network and knowledge grow like a snowball rolled over the ground after a winter storm.

The Snowball Technique can generate a long list of candidates for further meetings. That's OK. You can figure out which zone these folks belong in—some of them will be urgent Zone 1 people you have not thought to include or didn't know existed. Others will be Zone 3 people whose interviews can wait several months if needed as you work your way through the zones, although I recommend prioritizing wisdom-keepers. Either way, just keep asking the question. When you get to the point that you are no longer getting new names for your list, you know that the snowball is about as big as it is going to get. Just take your time and work your way systematically through the list. You will learn a lot, and fast.

Working with Your Assistant

If you are fortunate to have (or get to train) a trusted assistant to help you, this is a priceless gift and one for which to be grateful. This person can help to manage your calendar, represent your office, and manage incoming and outgoing communication for you while keeping an ear to the ground about the culture, people, processes, and resources across the organization. It is important to think about how to work effectively with such a critical person on your team. If you don't have an assistant now, this is still worthy of your consideration. As your career grows, you will likely have an opportunity to develop such a relationship, and if you enter a new role or organization with someone this talented already on your team, they are a tremendous resource to be respected, treated with dignity, and learned from as you onboard. Here are some key tips for working with an assistant:

- Respect him—he is a gatekeeper to your time and reputation and can make your life easier or harder. How you treat him matters.

- Meet with this person regularly, preferably at least weekly, but in the early days, daily touch-base meetings may be critical.

- Ask him what he thinks is most important for you to learn as you begin your work, then pay attention to what he tells you.

- Find out what his career goals are and support him in achieving those goals, even if you are training him for his next role.

- Set clear "rules of the road" for communication preferences on both sides. How do each of you like to receive information and questions? Do you prefer, texts, emails, or phone calls? Do you like lots of information, or brief lists of bullet points? Does your assistant like detailed direction, or general guidance and the opportunity to self-direct?

- Consider your assistant's judgement, independence, and skills for representing you. Ask him how he would handle some sample sticky situations and gauge your initial estimate of his judgment based on the responses. Then be upfront about the level of judgment and independence you'd like to see and tell him you will work with them to develop it. Be clear that it is an expectation.

- Regarding your calendar, ask your assistant what he is used to doing for others. Talk about parameters and details. Are there standing meetings or planning times that you put on your calendar on a regular basis? Do you like an hour to plan for the upcoming week on Friday afternoons? Do you pick your kids up from school at 3:30 on Tuesdays? Is Thursday always a date night with your spouse or partner? Make sure that your assistant knows about those things. Make a list of the things that cannot be "bumped" and those that can. Help your assistant prioritize—perhaps if your direct boss or the president of the company calls, you want to be interrupted in any circumstance. Conversely, if an intern or student wants to meet with you, they should expect it to take a few weeks to get scheduled. If you like a fifteen-minute transition between meetings, time to walk or drive between locations, or all standing meetings to default to twenty minutes in length, let your assistant know. I call these my "Calendaring Rules of the Road," and creating and communicating them does require a lot of attention to detail. It also requires a deep working knowledge of whatever calendar software you use, and it requires regular, dedicated time for you and your assistant to discuss what is working and what is not.

- As you are developing plans for getting to know people, enlisting your assistant to help with your schedule will be critical, and he or she will need to understand how to prioritize the meetings you plan. Ideally, you should involve your assistant in this planning, so he understands that he is an integral part of the process.

All this may sound like a lot, but I promise you, the investment of your time will be worth it!

The First 100 (or 365 or 730) Days

At this point, taking on a new role may seem like an impossible set of tasks, and I'll agree. The list of things to do is daunting. But it can be manageable if you stay organized, pace yourself, and keep perspective. I suggest thinking about your timeline in this way:

- Make a list of priority tasks for the first thirty days. These include meeting with Zone 1 Key Informants and taking care of any procedural, legal, financial, or other tasks. You may also find yourself dealing with anything that seems like it's "on fire" and in need of urgent your attention (this should be a short list, and you should think about what it takes for something to make it to that list). Of course, you'll include anything your boss asks you to address quickly in your priority tasks. And meeting with your assistant should be regular, frequent, and increasingly helpful to both of you.

- Next, make a list of tasks for days thirty-one through sixty. You may still be meeting with Zone 1 Key Informants and beginning to move into Zone 2. You are gathering information about the organization and have hopefully surfaced anything that's smoldering but not yet "on fire." Now is a good time to go back to the vision statement you presented during your interview, so you can update it based on what you now know. Set a mutually agreeable schedule for check-ins with your boss and ask for feedback about anything she or he sees that could be improved, as well as anything that has gone well so far. Don't forget to make time to take your assistant out to lunch and get his feedback on what is going well for him, what you can help with and anything he wishes you would do differently. And no, I am not advocating waiting for a year to do this—just make sure you are doing it by now and make it a regular part of your feedback strategy.

- Now make a list of tasks for days sixty-one through one hundred. By this point you should probably have finished your Zone 2 Key Informant meetings and begun moving into Zone 3. You should make a second set of revisions to your vision statement during this period. Settle into your day-to-day routine and begin to map out the work of your leadership if you are in a leadership role. If you are in a subject-matter-expert role (or a frontline contributor), you should have a handle on your day-to-day tasks and expectations. The tools you need to do your work should generally be in place. Check in again with your boss and see if the frequency of your meetings needs to be adjusted.

- From the hundred-day (or roughly three-month) period through six months, make a list of realistic things you can accomplish.

Limit your list to no more than three big goals (not counting day-to-day tasks), and make sure that one of those goals involves refining your vision and developing a communication strategy about your vision.

- From six through twelve months, you will be deepening your understanding of the organization and its culture, people, and resources. You will have developed a vision and timeline with strategies and tactics for implementing that vision. At this point in your tenure, you may be expected to communicate clearly about that vision and your plans for achieving it. People won't want to wait much longer (unless something like a pandemic intervenes) to see you start taking action and talking about your plans. Update your working list of things you want to accomplish, keeping it to no more than three big goals.

- Congratulations! At this point you will be approaching one year in your new role. As you approach this milestone, you are likely continuing to meet with Zone 3 people who are new to you, and you will have cemented a habit of meeting with your Zone 1 and Zone 2 people on a recurring basis. Make a list of three major accomplishments you want to achieve during your second year on the job and be thinking ahead to your Year 3 goals. Keep your list to three big things and keep moving forward.

- *Celebrate your accomplishments!* You have a lot to be proud of. Be sure to make time and space to pause and recognize how far you've come.

This is not an exhaustive list. But it will give you a rough framework for approaching the first thirty days through the first two years on the job.

Managing Your Time and Energy

In Chapter 11, we discussed managing your time and energy through the challenging offboarding and onboarding phase. Your time and energy management strategies are even more critical at this stage because your situation is no longer time-limited as it was when you were moving between roles. Now that you are in your new role for the long haul, you'll need to prioritize self-care to ensure you can thrive. Here are my best thoughts about creating lasting habits for your personal and professional well-being. You have heard these before, but I think they are so important that I will repeat them here:

- ✓ Don't forget to rest and exercise—put this on your calendar and give yourself some regular "off" time when you disconnect from electronics and decision-making. It makes a big difference.

- ✓ Talk to your personal stakeholders, particularly a spouse or partner if you have one, and others in your family. Ask how they are doing with the realities of your day-to-day life now that you are established in your new role.

- ✓ You cannot possibly do everything you imagine needs to be done, and some things will *not* get done. This is still true, and it always will be. Consider taking at least one meeting and one task off your plate every week. Decide to delegate those items, or just let them go.

- ✓ Set aside time each day to list three things for which you are grateful and three things you have learned. It's amazing how this habit can help you keep perspective.

- ✓ Be kind and gentle to yourself and those around you.

- ✓ Don't forget to rest and exercise. And REST some more.

Arriving at That Happy and Thriving Place

If you have made it this far with me in the Career Transitions Cycle, you have probably figured out that my model aims to move you back to the first stage, "Happy and Thriving." That is really the goal of this whole process. To determine when you've landed here, ask yourself periodically if your reasons for making your career move are being realized. Are you happier personally and professionally? Are you growing? Are you thriving, or just surviving? Those questions become touchstones for you to stay intentional about where you are, and when it's time to enter the cycle again.

When you do decide to move back through the Career Transitions Cycle, know that you have a road map, and every single time you do it, you will learn new things about yourself, what matters most to you, and how to manage change. Welcome to your DYNAMIC career! Here's to a long period of "Happy and Thriving."

CHAPTER 12 TOOL

Purpose

Use this interview guide to plan for conversations with key informants in your new organization.

Instructions

Decide who your "key informants" are as you get yourself onboarded, and then plan for a conversation with those people. I suggest that you develop a handful of interview questions for all key informants who are at a given level in the organization. This means a list for those above you, a list for those who will be reporting to you, and a list for those who are peers or colleagues.

Plan on 30 minutes per interview, and use your questions as a guide while giving the person you are interviewing time to add any information they think is important - what they share beyond your questions is often a gold mine!

These questions are not meant to be all-inclusive, and you should feel free to mix and match among my sample questions as you see fit. Choose three to five questions, and for each interview/meeting, ask the same questions of everyone on a given level. Then, let them talk about whatever else they want to share with you. You'll get some consistent information on important questions, but their unscripted answers will be informative.

Also, be sensitive to the concerns of those who will report to you. Sharing your questions ahead of time with them may help alleviate some anxiety about "meeting with the boss." Be sure to tell them you're just seeking to learn and that you are happy to hear about things beyond your questions; it's just a starting point for conversation.

Key Informant Interview Guide
Page 2

For those above you in the organization (those you report to and those they report to)

- What are the most important things that someone in my position should know about the organization and about my unit?
- What are the top three opportunities the organization and my unit should be looking at on the horizon?
- What are the top three things you want me to be focusing on for the next 90 days? The next year?
- How will you know and measure whether I have been successful in my new role?
- How do you like to receive information? Format (email, text, phone call), level of detail (bullet points, paragraphs, other) and frequency? What are key things I should always bring to you? What are key things I should not bring to you?
- Who are the Wisdom Keepers in the organization — those who know how things really operate, even if they are not in obvious positions of power or authority?
- Who else should I be talking with?

For those who will report to you (staff, team members, anyone you will be formally evaluating)

- Tell me about your job as you understand it.
- Do you have the tools and resources you need to do your job well?
- What are your primary career goals?
- What is most important to you that I pay attention to in the next 90 days? The next year?
- How will you know and measure whether I have been successful in my new role?
- Who are the Wisdom Keepers in the organization — those who know how things really operate, even if they are not in obvious positions of power or authority?
- Who else should I be talking with?

For peers, colleagues and others you want to listen to or gather input from

- What are the most important things you think someone in my position should be aware of about the organization and my unit?
- What are the top three things I should focus on for the next 90 days? The next year?
- What key partnerships should I be exploring?
- How will you know and measure whether I have been successful in my new role?
- How will I know if you think I should be doing something differently?
- Who are the Wisdom Keepers in the organization — those who know how things really operate, even if they are not in obvious positions of power or authority?
- Who else should I be talking with?

CHAPTER 12 – SUMMARY

Setting yourself up for success is a process that starts with learning about the organization, its people, and its resources. Using a systematic approach for this work will give you a deep understanding of your new professional home and how best to modify and realize your vision. Setting Up for Success is a process that can last months or years, but when you invest the time to do it right, you will soon find yourself right back at the Happy and Thriving stage, where you will hopefully stay for some time before it's time for another trip through the Career Transitions Cycle.

Core Concepts

- Coming into a new organization requires that you learn about its culture, people, and resources, as well as the processes for obtaining and managing those resources.

- People in your new organization will want to get to know you, and you will need and want to get to know them. Plan intentionally for doing this.

- Understand clearly who will be managing your calendar, and get to know them early, while setting up rules of the road for scheduling your time.

- An intentional plan for getting to know people is critical. As we discussed in Chapter 11, thinking of concentric "zones" of people will help you prioritize and strategize for communication and relationship-building.

- Key Informant interviews and Snowballing are two techniques that can help you learn and organize and prioritize your time. They can also create a very real sense that you are engaged and interested in those around you.

- If you are fortunate enough to have an assistant, learn how to work with them well, and support and value them for the people they are and the role they play in your success.

- Communicating about your vision and strategy is something that should take time. Don't be drawn into committing early unless there is a "burning platform" where a fire needs to be put out before you can move forward.

Key Takeaways

What are your Key Takeaways from this chapter? What did you learn, in your own words?

Very Next Actions

After reading this chapter, are there any Very Next Actions (VNAs) you need to take based on what you have learned?

VNA #1:

VNA #2:

PART 4:

Lifelong Context Development –
Along the Life Course

As you have seen by now, careers are dynamic, and they consistently exist in a cycle of transition (even if those cycles are long because of your personal and professional circumstances). However, these cycles exist in a larger context. Over the years of your life, your personal and professional goals, dreams, and wishes will evolve. Although your core values are likely to stay constant, your understanding of those values will likely mature over time.

This section of the book offers you a framework for understanding your career over the span of your professional lifetime—from the time you enter training until you create the capstone at the pinnacle of your work, whatever form that takes for you. This model is applicable across multiple job changes and even across multiple career changes, and it will help you plan and prepare for the steps you will need to take, the skills you will need to build, and the developmental tasks you will need to complete throughout a lifetime of professional engagement.

Three of my own life experiences have shaped this section of the book. The first is the fact that I am, at heart, a family physician. In my training, we learned about families, systems, and developmental tasks for individuals and for the families in which they exist. I was taught about developmental tasks for children, such as learning to smile, roll over, walk, tie shoes, and develop the language and social skills to attend school. In over thirty years of clinical practice, it became apparent to me that developmental tasks do not stop with childhood. Adults also cycle through developmental milestones. We must learn to handle money, to choose and hold a job, to enter deep adult relationships such as marriage or life partnerships, and with time and aging, we need to make sense and meaning of our lives. These patterns showed up in my clinical practice every day, and they fascinated me.

In graduate school, I encountered some wonderful teachers of sociology and human meaning-making. I had the opportunity to learn about the human life course, a sociologic concept developed and studied extensively by Dr. Glen Elder and others. That theory makes five key assumptions:[21]

- Human development and aging are lifelong processes.

- Individuals construct their own lives through the choices and actions they take within the opportunities and constraints of history and social circumstances.

- The life course of individuals is embedded and shaped by the historical times and places they experience over their lifetime.

- The developmental precursors and consequences of life transitions, events, and behavioral patterns vary according to their timing in a person's life.

- Human lives are interdependent, and social and historical influences are shaped by this network of shared relationships.

---

[21] Elder, Glen H., Monica K. Johnson, and Robert Crosnoe. 2003. *The Emergence and Development of Life Course Theory* in <u>Handbook of the Life Course</u> (Jeylan T. Mortimer and Michael J. Shanahan, Eds.). New York: Kluwer Academic Publishers.

I have used these assumptions as foundational pieces for the Life Course of a Professional Career component of my Professional Careers by Design™ model, and they are useful for putting career development in context and for helping professionals map successful, satisfying, and meaningful careers. I want to also acknowledge the work of another author whose approach to life stages shaped the development of this material. Dr. Joan Borysenko, a noted biologist, psychologist, and expert on the integration of mind and body in personal growth, wrote the book, *A Woman's Book of Life: The Biology, Psychology, and Spirituality of the Feminine Life Cycle.*[22] This book examines the stages of women's lives and the developmental tasks associated with each of them, and it was important to my own life and professional work. Dr. Borysenko articulates that people who understand these stages and their associated tasks can grow intentionally over the course of their lives. Her approach was instrumental in helping me become intentional about my own life choices, and I hope my application of it in this section of the book will help you too.

Over the course of my coaching career, I have observed patterns in the timing, shared experiences, and the social and historical context of my clients' lives. Those patterns shape individuals' sense of agency and their ability to make decisions about their own life and its evolution. As I have noted the emerging patterns, I have adapted ideas from human development, the Life Course Theory, and the developmental tasks approach used by Dr. Borysenko to the evolution of individuals and their professional careers.

Like the Career Transitions Cycle, the Life Course of a Professional Career is broken into stages, and each stage has developmental tasks to be accomplished and key markers of transition between stages. For each stage, I will also suggest resources and strategies that can help you meet those

---

[22] Borysenko, Joan MD. 1996. *A Woman's Book of Life: The Biology, Psychology, and Spirituality of the Feminine Life Cycle.* New York: The Berkley Publishing Group.

developmental tasks and make those transitions. You already have your road map from one job to the next. This section will help you map your progress through your entire career, from exhilarating beginning to proud and satisfying capstone.

13

The Life Course of a Career

Stages of a Career

Let's start with a high-level look at the phases and stages of a professional career, so you stay oriented as we dig into each. Figure 5 illustrates the stages I have had the privilege of watching over many hours of coaching as people grew through them.

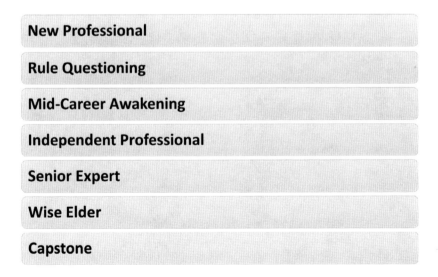

New Professional

Rule Questioning

Mid-Career Awakening

Independent Professional

Senior Expert

Wise Elder

Capstone

Figure 5: Developmental Stages of a Career

In this section of the book, I'll help you understand what happens in each of these parts of a career, over the course of a lifetime. We will discuss key developmental growth tasks that need to be accomplished, as well as self-care and other practices that will help you navigate the arc of your career.

It's important to know that there are many ways to move through these stages and phases.

- You may have one career over the course of your lifetime, enabling you to move through these stages sequentially, ending at the capstone and planning your formal retirement.

- You might have multiple careers, and thus move through these stages sequentially and intentionally for each career. A capstone in one career could be followed by training for the next.

- You could also define your career as entrepreneurship, for example. You might start and close or sell several companies, and move through all these stages, or you move through only some of them before leaping to another business (or even another career) that lands you somewhere in a new cycle.

There is no one right way to move through these stages, and your path may not be linear at all. I consider a "professional cycle" to be a complete pass through all the stages described above. You may have one of these cycles in your lifetime, or more than one.

I'll share a story from my own life that might help explain how I think about this. I once had the privilege of attending a jazz set at Preservation Hall in New Orleans. This was my first experience of live jazz, and the average age of the musicians on stage must have been over seventy-five. The air was thick with a blue and hazy smoke that some of you might recognize, and a pungent smell. I realized that the source of that smoke was the musicians on stage, who were partaking of a substance that is known to "prolong their personal minute," stretching their experience of time in a way that—as was explained to me later by a true jazz aficionado—would "allow them to play more notes in between the notes." The prolongation of that "personal minute" was a new concept to me. Time is not always what we think it is, and how we move through it depends on our circumstances.

How does this relate to career stages and a lifetime of professional work? I tell this story to remind you (and myself) that our own experience of time, its path and the role that timing and sequence play for each of us is different. Our careers are often not linear, and we typically spend more or less time in each job than we expect. That's OK.

Work and Career in the 21st Century

Varied and flexible careers are the norm now more than ever. In the United States, the average worker has twelve jobs throughout a lifetime,[23] and nearly 30 percent of those aged twenty-five to forty-four years who change jobs will change professional fields completely (for example, moving from teaching to running a florist business).[24] However, the stages and phases I describe in this section of the book still work, however your jobs and career unfold. What's important is you understand them, so you can place them in the context of your life and leverage them for the most satisfying career possible. Let's get started by learning more about each of these phases and stages, so you have the rest of the tools you need for your intentionally designed career.

---

[23] Boskamp, Elise. "21 Crucial Career Change Statistics [2023]: How Often Do People Change Jobs?" Zippia.Com. Zippia: The Career Expert, February 9, 2023. https://www.zippia.com/advice/career-change-statistics/.

[24] Team, EdX. "EdX Survey Finds that about 1/3 of Americans Ages 25 – 44 Have Completely Changed Fields Since Starting Their First Job Post-College." EdX Blog. EdX, July 10, 2018. https://blog.edx.org/edx-survey-finds-1-3-americans-ages-25-44-completely-changed-fields-since-starting-first-job-post-college.

CHAPTER 13 – SUMMARY

Careers occur in predictable stages, with definable milestones and strategies that help guide development. Understanding the Life Course of a Career, and the ways in which our conceptions of work change over time will help you manage your path through a career over time.

Core Concepts

- The Life Course Model can be applied to career design. It is a framework for understanding the arc of a career over time and planning ahead for that trajectory.

- There are key developmental tasks that adults must accomplish as they progress through the stages of a career. Intentional strategies from the Professional Careers by Design™ Model, as well as sound self-care and other practices can help navigate even the most complex of career paths.

- Our perceptions of work and career, and those of society in general, change over time as well, and shape the ways in which we make career choices.

Key Takeaways

What are your Key Takeaways from this chapter? What did you learn, in your own words?

Very Next Actions

After reading this chapter, are there any Very Next Actions (VNAs) you need to take based on what you have learned?

VNA #1:

VNA #2:

Design Your Outcomes First – Crafting a Capstone Plan

If You Don't Know Where You Are Going, It's Hard to Get There

You might think that starting by thinking about the "end" of your career is counterintuitive, but Steven Covey's idea of starting with the end in mind[25] is a good one. It's easy to just stumble through your career and take the opportunities that arise, but if you take this approach, you are likely to find yourself in your senior career without a plan for what comes next before you know it. The whole point of this book—and of this section of the book in particular—is to help you replace a haphazard approach with something **intentional.** The reason to do so is that this approach can provide a path to far fewer regrets and far greater success and satisfaction. That's why I'm going to encourage you to develop what I call your Capstone Plan.

---

[25] Covey, Stephen R. 2020. *The 7 Habits of Highly Effective People*. 3rd ed. New York: Simon & Schuster.

Key Elements of a Capstone Plan

Your Capstone Plan should be developed early, even during training, and updated regularly. You should revisit it whenever you update your what-matters-most-to-you list from Chapter 1 and use it to move through each stage with intention, so you advance toward what you want to do, learn, or focus on in the coming stages of your life. Having a Capstone Plan is not a one-time task, and it has both personal and professional dimensions. It's an iterative process that builds as you go through life. As with my other models, it starts with some key questions and considerations. These questions may sound familiar, from our work on the Discernment process in Part 2 of this book.

- Who am I outside of work?

    - What are my hobbies?

    - What are my passions?

    - What routines and activities provide structure for my days, both at work and at home?

- What do I imagine wanting to do at the end of my current professional cycle?

    - Encore Career

    - Altruism

    - Retirement

    - Something else

- Who will be affected by my planning for the end of this cycle?

- What do my personal stakeholders want at the end of this professional cycle? What do they want along the way?

- What do they want or hope for me?
- What do they want or hope for themselves?

- Energy assessment
  - What is my level of energy and enthusiasm for continuing to stay in this cycle?
  - What is my level of energy and enthusiasm for bringing this cycle to a close?
  - Which energy level is greater right now?
  - What am I ready, willing, and able to do with this energy assessment information?

- What is my transition plan?
  - What work do I want to finish in this professional cycle?
  - What work do I hope someone else will carry on?
  - Who do I believe will (or may) carry on that work?
  - How do I help those people get ready?
  - What will onboarding and offboarding from this cycle look like?
  - What concrete steps do I need to put in place for my next steps?
    - More training or education
    - Financial planning
    - Legal planning
    - Administrative details for the handoff

- How do I want to communicate about this right now? (Review the section on communicating about onboarding and offboarding decisions in Chapter 11 for some tips about how to think about this.)
    - To those in my personal list of stakeholders
    - To those in my professional world
    - To anyone else

As you go through this exercise, you might realize you don't have all these answers, but it's OK. Thinking about these questions long before you get to the end of a professional cycle will help you stay intentional about all the decisions you make.

With these questions in mind to frame your planning and thinking about your career as a series of stages and phases, let's look at each stage of the Life Course of a Career.

CHAPTER 14 TOOL

Capstone Planner

Purpose

This tool will help you plan for the Capstone stage of your career, even many years before you arrive at that point. It's never too soon to start!

Instructions

Use this worksheet as a guide to think about how you want to plan for the time when your current career has come to a close, and how you want your life to be at the end of this professional cycle. Feel free to add your own questions. Update your answers at least once a year and any time your life circumstances change in a significant way.

Date completed:

Notes about my current circumstances:

What is your current situation? Are you happy and fulfilled? Is a change in order? Are there stakeholder concerns, curveballs to consider or other significant issues you should take into account?

What is my current stage of career?

Trainee   Early Career   Mid-Career   Senior Career   Capstone

Capstone Planner
Page 2

- **Who am I outside of work?**
  - What are my hobbies?
  - What are my passions?
  - What routines and activities provide structure for my days, both at work and at home?

- **What do I imagine wanting to do at the end of my current professional cycle?**
  - Encore career
  - Altruism
  - Retirement
  - Something else

- **Who will be affected by my planning for the end of this cycle?**
  - What do my personal stakeholders want at the end of this professional cycle?
  - What do they want along the way?
  - What do they want or hope for me?
  - What do they want or hope for themselves?

- **Energy assessment**
  - What is my level of energy and enthusiasm for continuing to stay in this cycle?
  - What is my level of energy and enthusiasm for bringing this cycle to a close?
  - Which energy level is greater right now?
  - What am I ready, willing and able to do with this energy assessment information?

- **What is my transition plan?**
  - What work do I want to finish in this professional cycle?
  - What work do I hope someone else will carry on?
  - Who do I believe will (or may) carry on that work?
  - How do I help those people get ready?
  - What will onboarding and offboarding from this cycle look like?
  - What concrete steps do I need to put in place for my next steps?
    - More training or education
    - Financial planning
    - Legal planning
    - Administrative details for the handoff

- **How do I want to communicate about this transition right now? (Review the section on communicating about onboarding and offboarding in Chapter 11 for some tips about how to think about this.)**
  - To those in my personal list of stakeholders
  - To those in my professional world
  - To anyone else

CHAPTER 14 – SUMMARY

Beginning with a plan for where you want to end up in the Capstone stage of your career can seem counterintuitive. The earlier in your career you can envision the roadmap, the easier you will find it to navigate the transitions. Having a Capstone Plan can help you think ahead, even if you are just entering a career.

Core Concepts

- The key questions to ask in making a Capstone Plan are based in that process of discernment we explored in Part 2 of the book.

- You don't have to have all the answers at the beginning. Some answers will only become clear over time. It's OK to start where you are and fill in the gaps as you go.

Key Takeaways

What are your Key Takeaways from this chapter? What did you learn, in your own words?

Very Next Actions

After reading this chapter, are there any Very Next Actions (VNAs) you need to take based on what you have learned?

VNA #1:

VNA #2:

The Trainee Phase – Entering a Career

P rofessional careers officially begin during the training process, though many people would say that all the education and acculturation that happens before professional training begins also shapes the entire career. That is correct, but for the purposes of this book, we will focus on the training that officially signals entry into a profession. That training could occur within the formal education system, but it could also include apprenticeships, mentorship into a creative field, and many other potential means of entry.

If you are a trainee or learner in a professional pathway, you have essentially declared a wish or desire to pursue that professional work, a willingness to work with accepted teachers or masters in the field, and an openness to being a student, apprentice, or other type of learner. The key to this way of thinking is that you, as a trainee, want to learn about both the details of the work and the culture and behavioral expectations for that work. You agree to submit to the tutelage of the established teachers or masters of the work. You are willing to put in the time, and usually are prepared to pay for the training and to delay gratification in the form of monetary reward and autonomy until your training is complete.

Developmental Tasks

Key developmental tasks in this stage include:

- Publicly declaring a desire to learn and willingness to enter training as prescribed by the profession.

- Undergoing the actual work of training.

- Acculturating to the behavioral expectations of the profession.

- Handling your own doubts about your choices when they arise. This is often the first major challenge of intentionally designing a career: developing a means to manage this doubt.

- Delaying gratification in terms of monetary benefit, autonomy over your own time, and public recognition of your ability to do the work.

You may have your first experience of impostor syndrome as you enter this process. This concept, originally defined as "an internal experience of intellectual phoniness,"[26] was first described as an experience of high-functioning professional women. More current thinking (including in my own experience with clients in my coaching practice) recognizes that this phenomenon occurs regardless of gender.[27]

Impostor syndrome is commonly experienced as a sense of not being good enough or performing well enough to be in the current position held.

---

[26] Clance, Pauline R., and Suzanne Imes. "The Imposter Phenomenon in High Achieving Women: Dynamics and Therapeutic Interventions." *Psychotherapy: Theory, Research and Practice 15*, no. 3 (1978): 241-247. Accessed June 25, 2023. https://doi.org/https://psycnet.apa.org/doi/10.1037/h0086006.

[27] Bravata, Dena M., Sharon A. Watts, Autumn L. Keefer, Divya K. Madhusudhan, Katie T. Taylor, Dani M. Clark, Ross S. Nelson, Kevin O. Cokley, and Heather K. Hagg. "Prevalence, Predictors, and Treatment of Impostor Syndrome: A Systematic Review." *Journal of General Internal Medicine 35*, no. 4 (2020): 1252-1275. Accessed June 25, 2023. https://doi.org/10.1007%2Fs11606-019-05364-1.

It also comes with a sense of anxiety about being "found out" to be not good enough. It is important to note that impostor syndrome is complex, and it may not be the appropriate label for the sense of "not belonging" that can be experienced by racial and ethnic minorities, women, and other marginalized people in settings where systemic bias occurs.[28] Overcoming a sense of not belonging is both a developmental task for many trainees (and others along the course of their careers) and for organizations seeking to address systemic bias. Dealing with this phenomenon is an added burden that professionals from marginalized groups should not have to face.

How Do I Know I Am Ready to Move to the Next Career Stage?

Completion of the Trainee Phase is usually recognized in some public way. Either the mentor or guide ushers the trainee into public presentation of their work, or there is a formal and ritualized graduation process that tells the world this person has met the requirements to work in the profession, and there may be some form of imprimatur bestowed. It is important to note that this may be the last time in an individual's life that there is formal recognition of professional transition. That becomes important in the next stage of professional life, as you will see.

Strategies for Success

Self-Care Strategies

Trainees can support their own growth and development in many ways, but self-care habits are critical. When self-care is not a priority, the training process can be more challenging than it otherwise would be. If you are a trainee, strategies that can help include:

---

[28] Tulshyan, Ruchika, and Jodi-Ann Burey. "Stop Telling Women They Have Imposter Syndrome." *Harvard Business Review* (Boston), February 11, 2021. https://hbr.org/2021/02/stop-telling-women-they-have-imposter-syndrome.

- A good physical self-care routine that includes exercise, sleep, and healthy nutrition
- A network of family, friends, and confidants with whom to talk about what is happening as your training progresses.
- A spiritual source of support if that is important to you.
- A mental health support system if appropriate

Intentional Career Design Strategies

This is also a perfect point to start using the What Matters Most to You exercise found in Chapter 1. This foundational self-awareness exercise can help navigate stress and doubt and remind you of why you got into your training process in the first place. I strongly recommend repeating this exercise at least annually, and whenever stress or doubts arise about the choices you have made.

Other Tips

In addition to the basic self-care ideas above, this is a good stage of life in which to seek professional guidance about finance from trusted professionals or family members, so you can navigate the delayed financial autonomy with as little hardship as possible.

These strategies do not guarantee success by themselves—training is hard work, and the learning and growing you signed up for will challenge you. But these supportive strategies can set up a healthy approach to the training stage and make it more likely that you can thrive during this process.

CHAPTER 15 – SUMMARY

The Trainee stage is the entry point into professional life. It is an exciting time, though it can also be stressful. But it's a great time to begin practicing Intentional Career Design habits that will support a thriving journey through this stage, and all the stages to come.

Core Concepts

- The Trainee stage begins with a public declaration that you want to learn the skills and behavioral expectations of a specific type of work.

- Key developmental tasks in this stage include willingness to do the work of training, including the process of acculturating to the expectations of the work, learning to manage doubts about your career choice, and learning to manage any delayed gratification that is required.

- Strategies for success in this stage include a good self-care routine and potentially seeking formal financial guidance from a trusted advisor.

- Intentional Career Design strategies for this stage include developing the habit of using the What Matters Most to You exercise to understand your choices and navigate doubts and updating your list at least annually and anytime significant changes happen in your life.

Key Takeaways

What are your Key Takeaways from this chapter? What did you learn, in your own words?

Very Next Actions

After reading this chapter, are there any Very Next Actions (VNAs) you need to take based on what you have learned?

VNA #1:

VNA #2:

Early Career Part 1 – New Professional Stage

This career stage begins when your training is complete and your first formal work in the profession begins. As an Early Career Professional, you have gained the approval of those you trained under and have been designated as having achieved the skills and integration of professional expectations necessary to the profession. As a newly minted professional, you are expected to abide by the rules of socialization that govern the field. You may find yourself accepting your first professional role in the same organization where you trained (which presents a special set of challenges we will discuss shortly).

Developmental Tasks

In order to grow and develop from this point, these key tasks must be addressed:

- Differentiating oneself and moving from the role of trainee—under supervision and with others ultimately responsible for outcomes of performance—to the role of a working professional responsible for their own performance, time management, and success.

- Managing impostor syndrome if it rears its head. In the early career stage, impostor syndrome shows up any time you change roles, gain authority, or take on a new task. It is also possible that a sense of not belonging may actually be the result of systemic bias within the system. Learning to manage and navigate that systemic problem as a professional, rather than as a trainee, is a key skill for this stage.

- Learning the organizational and professional measures of success and incorporating them into habitual work patterns. This is a key task for new professionals. Until this stage in a career, the entire educational system (at least in the Western world) is prescriptive—the teacher tells the learner what must be done to pass a course, and the learner performs at her best. That process has likely worked well to date for a new professional, but the work world is different. The metrics for success are often inexplicit or vague, and sometimes they change without warning. Navigating communication about these metrics is vital to succeeding in this career stage.

- Wisely saying yes to opportunities. Learning what to say yes to is a key part of this career stage. If a new professional is fortunate enough to have mentors or allies, those allies may bring forth many opportunities for engagement within the organization, such as committee work, new tasks and increased visibility through meetings and introductions. They may even provide sponsorship, which is a step beyond mentorship—sponsors put the new professional's name forward for awards, leadership roles, and other types of recognition. The new professional must talk with the mentor or sponsor about the timing of these opportunities and the volume of them that can be realistically accepted.

How Do I Know I Am Ready to Move to the Next Career Stage?

Completion of this stage is not as clearly delineated as the end of the Trainee stage. In my coaching practice, the first sign I see is often that the person I'm coaching is frustrated by the rules for success or figuring out that those rules don't fit their goals very well. Professionals approaching the end of this stage also have been in their role long enough to know the basics, and any impostor syndrome may be easing.

If training occurred in the same organization as the first employment, this stage may take a bit longer. The relationships in this case are deeper, and others may continue to see the former learner as a trainee, delaying their acceptance of this person in the role of new professional. While the shift from trainee to professional is a big leap for anyone, it typically takes longer if people have preconceived notions of who the individual has been, rather than who they are becoming.

Strategies for Success

Self-Care Strategies

I know it's redundant, but my list of self-care steps still applies, perhaps even more so in the early years of your career. I'll reiterate that list here:

- A good physical self-care routine that includes exercise, sleep, and a healthy diet.
- A network of family, friends, and confidants with whom to talk about your experience as a new professional.
- A spiritual source of support if that is important to you.
- A mental health support system if appropriate.

In addition, self-care includes finding someone you trust with whom you can safely discuss any questions about the organization, and with whom you can review the opportunities that come your way. That sounding board can be critical to helping you avoid overcommitment, which is itself a task of self-care.

Intentional Career Design Strategies

This is a perfect time to review those Hip Pocket Questions from Chapter 4.

1. Revisiting the What Matters Most to You exercise at least annually should be an ingrained habit by now. That exercise is the first step in the Hip Pocket Questions—Know Yourself.

2. Talk with your stakeholders (the people in your life who are affected by your career decisions). Find out what is important to them at this stage of your career and consider the alignment between what matters to you and what matters to them. It may be the first time since you completed training that they can have a voice in your career decisions. Listen to them, but don't forget it's up to you to decide whether they get a vote in your choices.

3. In addition, work with your trusted mentor or sponsor to ensure you are clear on your organization's values, pressures, and opportunities. Ask that mentor to help you understand your place in the organizational system, and to help you understand both who has visible power and who has hidden power within that system. These discussions can be invaluable.

4. Review whether any major misalignments emerge in the first three steps. If some do, you may want to go back to Chapter 8 to determine if you need to stay or go and see if you are in the "Search Targeting" stage of your Career Transitions Cycle. Hopefully, at this early stage in your career, there won't

be major misalignments, but that doesn't mean no action is needed. You can review the Four Es exercise in Chapter 7 and look for opportunities to grow.

5. Make some decisions about ways you want to grow, what you want to say yes to and what you still need to learn in the process.

The important part about these Hip Pocket Questions is that, at any point where you are questioning your decisions, you can run back through them and reassess. It's a habit worth developing, and it will serve you at every stage of your career.

Other Tips

This is a stage where you may feel untethered. It may be the first time you have ever been without a defined external goal to mark your success or completion of a segment of your career. In my coaching practice, the first hint I hear that a client is struggling with these feelings comes when they ask, "How do I know what to do next?" or "Is this all there is? I don't have a goal or an endpoint, and thirty (or forty or fifty) years of this just seems depressing."

If you are struggling with this issue, it's a good time to seek out a coach with whom you can discuss your career trajectory. If you are dealing with depression, anxiety, or other mental health concerns related to this (or to anything else), it's also critical to seek out a trained mental health professional to help you integrate these feelings. These questions and feelings are common, and people do make peace with them over time. It's also a common time to need professional support. Don't be afraid to ask for it.

CHAPTER 16 – SUMMARY

The New Professional stage can be exciting at first, but it can also become frustrating. Know that transition tasks you may encounter, such as managing impostor syndrome, are common developmental issues and not a personal fault or flaw. Treat them as learning opportunities that will help you be intentional about planning the career you want and then master the key skills needed to get you there. Remember that your career is a long game, not a sprint. Being intentional and recognizing that you are growing will help you navigate this stage.

Core Concepts

- The New Professional stage begins when you start your first formal job in the field after your training is complete. It's an exciting time with some developmental challenges.

- If your first job is at the same place where you trained, your progress through this stage may take longer, both because of how you look at yourself and how others see you as you transition from trainee to professional.

- Key Developmental Tasks in this stage include differentiating from a trainee to a working professional, managing imposter syndrome, learning the rules for success in your organization, and learning to say yes to opportunities that serve your goals.

- Strategies for Success in this stage include good physical and mental health self-care practices and finding a trusted mentor who can help you learn the ropes in your organization and vet the opportunities that come your way.

- Intentional Career Design steps for this stage include revisiting the Hip Pocket Questions for yourself, your stakeholders, and your organization. It's also important to ask for the help of professionals, including mental health professionals if needed, and/or a coach for developmental support at this stage of your career.

Key Takeaways

What are your Key Takeaways from this chapter? What did you learn, in your own words?

Very Next Actions

After reading this chapter, are there any Very Next Actions (VNAs) you need to take based on what you have learned?

VNA #1:

VNA #2:

Early Career Part 2 – Questioning

The Questioning stage could also be called "Questioning it All." When my coaching clients reach this stage, they have figured out that the rules for success they have worked so hard to learn and integrate may not work for them and their career goals. If you are in this stage, you may be questioning why you took your current job in the first place, or whether to stay. It's a time when you may move into the "Search Targeting" stage of the Career Transition Cycle (Part 3, Chapter 8) if you identify a need to create better alignment with your goals or your stakeholders' needs. Impostor syndrome may begin to recede, although recall that this experience is exacerbated and complicated by systemic bias; if it becomes clear that organizational bias is an issue for you, it may feel like it's time to leave the organization.

People at the Questioning stage are often overcommitted. Common statements I hear from clients at this point in their career journey include:

- "I'm ready to look for something else."
- "I'm just not fitting in here."
- "Can I make this work, and if so, what do I need to do?"
- "Can you help me figure out what to take off my plate?"

Let's explore what's going on for professionals in this phase.

Developmental Tasks

Key developmental tasks for this stage include:

- Questioning everything! This *is* the developmental task for this stage. Learning how to question things effectively, to either bring about change, or collect enough data to let you know you need to leave, is the skill to build. Trusted mentors or a professional coach can be a big help in building this skill.

- Learning to say no effectively. Overcommitment is often in full bloom during this stage. In his book *Stop Competing and Start Winning: The Business of Coaching* my good friend and colleague Leo Hopf says that the task here is to "learn to say 'no' with a period after it so that you can say 'yes' with an exclamation point!"[29] He's right, and I call this "learning how to say the strategic 'no.'" It's strategic because it allows you say yes to the opportunities that align best with your personal and professional goals, the needs of your stakeholders and the perspective of your organization (do you hear the Hip Pocket Questions here???). Gaining the ability to discern the difference is a key task of this stage.

- Achieving some early-career wins. This can mean winning some pivotal cases if you are an attorney, publishing some papers or getting a grant if you are a scientist or other researcher, and selling a piece of software or a significant work of art if you are a technology or creative arts professional. These are measures of success that are more specific to your profession than your job and organization. They demonstrate to others inside and outside your organization that you are good at what you do. This kind of success occurs on a public stage where it's important to show

---

[29] Launiere, Beth, and Leo Hopf. 2020. *Stop Competing and Start Winning: The Business of Coaching*. Salt Lake City, UT: Leo Hopf. Quoted with permission. Electronic permission on file.

your skills. Additionally, the need to do this relates to my next point.

- Rejecting premature career advancement. One scenario where it's critical to say "no" is any situation in which you are offered a senior leadership or administrative role before you are ready for it. It's very flattering to get an offer like this early in your career. It's also easy to misunderstand the reality of those jobs and the degree to which your time will be taken up with administrative tasks, rather than the core professional work in which you trained. As someone who made this mistake early in her career, I can report that such a move can seriously derail your professional success OR pose a serious risk of overcommitment (or BOTH). Trying to do all the administrative tasks and all the professional tasks appropriate to the role while developing early career professional success can be a recipe for career disaster. Folks in my coaching practice who take such roles too early end up seriously overcommitted, and they often come to me for help rebalancing their portfolio of professional work versus administrative work without derailing their career, their health, or their relationships.

How Do I Know I Am Ready to Move to the Next Career Stage?

If you complete the developmental tasks outlined above, you will deepen your understanding of what you love most about the work you do—as well as the things you don't enjoy. Your early successes are visible beyond your workplace and they bring more opportunities, but you are more discerning about what you agree to do. You increasingly recognize that the external measures of success you fought to achieve in your early career may not always serve you personally. If this sounds familiar, you are probably ready to move on to what's next.

Strategies for Success

Self-Care Strategies

I won't repeat the list, but self-care strategies are critical here. Remember that it's OK to ask for help and support in achieving these strategies. Saying no strategically and effectively is a critical part of self-care. Practice taking something off your calendar each week that does not align with your goals and needs. Make a list of criteria that must be met before you will say "yes" to an opportunity—these criteria can be both professional and personal in nature. Practice saying no to things that do not meet those standards and revise your criteria every six months as your career develops.

Intentional Career Design Strategies

As always, keep your list of what matters most to you current. Consider looking at the Stay/Go Grid discussed in Chapter 6 and evaluating the pros and cons of staying, going, thriving, and surviving. Also consider using the Four Es exercise from Chapter 7 to figure out how to improve alignment where you are, or to discern what kind of position you should look for if you decide it's time for something new.

Other Tips

This is a time to celebrate some of your career successes and the completion of the early phase of your career. You likely have a clearer understanding of both your personal and professional goals than ever before, and you are probably practicing the skills of time management, commitment management, and saying yes and no to opportunities in a way that will contribute to your ongoing success.

CHAPTER 17 – SUMMARY

Figuring out how to question the assumptions you have made—and those your organization makes on your behalf—can be empowering. It can also be frustrating, and learning to question effectively is a critical component of intentionally managing your career. The temptation to take on too much is high at this stage but learning skills and managing the developmental tasks at this level will set you up for moving toward the mid-career stage and the emerging independence likely to come.

Core Concepts

- The Questioning process begins with a growing desire to question core assumptions you and your organization have made about what success looks like. Alignment between the two is either coming into focus at this stage or falling apart. If you are experiencing misalignment, you may start questioning whether to continue in your current setting or move onto something new.

- Key Developmental Tasks in this stage include learning how to question the assumptions and rules of success effectively—within the organization and within yourself—learning how to say "no" strategically, focusing on achieving some early wins related to your professional work, and avoiding premature acceptance of administrative roles.

- Strategies for Success in this stage include routine self-care and practicing concrete actions that allow you to say the "strategic no," and celebrating some of those early successes you're racking up. The ritual of celebration helps to mark the milestones along the way.

- Intentional Career Design steps for this stage include maintaining your Top Ten List of what matters most to you, reviewing the Four Es exercise and the Stay/Go Grid to evaluate opportunities to enhance your situation either at your current organization or beyond it.

Key Takeaways

What are your Key Takeaways from this chapter? What did you learn, in your own words?

Very Next Actions

After reading this chapter, are there any Very Next Actions (VNAs) you need to take based on what you have learned?

VNA #1:

VNA #2:

Mid-Career Part 1 – Awakening to Agency

As you enter this stage, you are beginning to accept that the rules and assumptions you made when you began your career do not apply perfectly to your current situation, and they may seem to be applied unfairly in your workplace. You have asked questions and made choices based on your own needs and the needs of your stakeholders at this season of your life. You have a deepening understanding of your own goals and the sense of increasing success you are developing in your organization and beyond.

As a mid-career professional, you may be offered your first leadership roles, and you may now be ready to balance the need for your own success as a frontline contributor with the need and desire to take on leadership and administrative roles that allow you to have influence over the success of others. You begin to believe that you have agency or self-efficacy to make decisions about your own career path, and you have the confidence to pursue those decisions even if others disagree with your choice. You understand and continue to practice saying the "strategic no," but you are also prioritizing decisions that serve you and your stakeholders in a meaningful way. This is the "strategic yes," and it's a hallmark of this career stage.

Developmental Tasks

Developmental tasks in this stage focus on your ability to make decisions and take the risk of going against expectations. Some of these specific tasks include:

- Learning what to say yes to and being able to do so because you have said no to the things that do not serve you. This is the art of the "strategic yes."

- Clarification of professional goals for mid-life, particularly consideration of competing professional and personal interests. This is the peak period for work-life alignment questions to come up.

- Learning to effectively manage personal responses to potentially unfair application of rules for success (when the meritocracy doesn't seem to work).

- Beginning to mentor early career professionals in the power structure, values, expectations, and other parameters of the organizational culture while also helping mentees understand the need to practice the "strategic no."

How Do I Know I Am Ready to Move to the Next Stage?

As a coach, my clues that someone is moving through this stage and onto the next arise when I hear them say, "I let go of this committee," or "I have a succession plan for this role," while they also begin to articulate a clear vision for their career trajectory, including leadership roles.

If you have reached this point, you will be doing more of the work you choose and less of work that is assigned to you by others. You may have experienced a work-related crisis, an unfair application of expectations, or other career-related traumatic events, and you are beginning to come through that and make your own choices. Finally, leadership roles are becoming more comfortable, and a decision about whether to continue serving as a frontline contributor in your profession or move into full-time administration may be at hand. These are signs you are ready for the next stage.

Strategies for Success

Self-Care Strategies

The same physical, mental, and spiritual self-care measures apply here, as at all stages. In addition, a clear act of self-care in this stage is the ability to choose what you are saying the "strategic yes" to. Choosing those things that align to your goals and values is easier in this stage, and it is a consummately empowering thing to be able to do.

Intentional Career Design Strategies

In this stage, staying connected with your What Matters Most to You list is by now a habit, and one that you practice and keep up-to-date regularly. Deciding whether to consider leadership roles or to move up within or outside your organization are again informed by the Stay/Go Grid and the Four Es exercise. It can also be helpful to begin to think about the idea of legacy and what you want your overall career arc to have accomplished. It's not too early to consider these points and begin planning an intentional approach to achieving what you hope for.

Other Tips

This is a great time to reconnect with your financial planner. If you don't already have one, you'll want to form a relationship with a legal advisor who can help you with retirement, estate, and end-of-life planning. Yes, it's not too early to think about those things as well. (I hope that you began to build this team and consider these issues earlier than this stage of your career. Early career, even the day you receive your first paycheck, is not too soon.)

CHAPTER 18 – SUMMARY

This first part of the mid-career stage involves integrating the learnings from early career and moving into self-efficacy to design your own career. It may be the first portion of your work life in which you fully believe that you can intentionally design your life. Welcome to the fun!

Core Concepts

- The Mid-Career Awakening Stage begins with having successfully completed a period of questioning and reorienting your career goals. You have come to recognize that you have the agency or self-efficacy to make those choices for yourself.

- Key Developmental Tasks in this stage include learning to say the "strategic yes," clarifying personal and professional goals as part of an intentionally designed life, managing and moving through unfair or traumatic workplace experiences in a professional way, and beginning to mentor others.

- Strategies for Success in this stage include my standard self-care recommendations, as well as consulting with financial planners and legal advisors as appropriate to your personal and professional needs.

- Intentional Career Design steps for this stage include keeping your Top Ten List of what matters most to you up-to-date, particularly as you gain clarity and confidence in your ability to make decisions. The Stay/Go Grid and the Four Es may also be helpful. Finally, it's not too early to begin planning for your career's legacy. What outcomes do you want to ensure you achieve?

Key Takeaways

What are your Key Takeaways from this chapter? What did you learn, in your own words?

Very Next Actions

After reading this chapter, are there any Very Next Actions (VNAs) you need to take based on what you have learned?

VNA #1:

VNA #2:

Mid-Career Part 2 – Independent Professional

I f you have reached the Independent Professional stage of mid-career, you have developed clarity regarding your goals, both personal and professional. You are comfortable articulating what you hope to do, and you can clearly tell others what you are not planning to accomplish. You have been recognized for significant success well beyond your organization, and you have begun thinking seriously about how to craft a succession plan for handing off your professional endeavors. You may be offered a mid-level leadership role and successfully undertake it, and you are comfortable balancing your time between frontline contribution and leadership roles.

Developmental Tasks

Developmental tasks in this stage focus on taking stock of success and planning for what's next. Specific tasks include:

- Planning for completion of your professional endeavors. Is there work still to be done that you feel strongly about completing yourself. This is a perfect time to focus on that. And will there be work to be done when you step away? If yes, determine who will take it over and whether you can or should step back at some point to allow that person to move forward without you.

- Succeeding at leadership roles and the continuing the balance of frontline contribution and leadership; beginning to consider stepping out of frontline contribution roles.

- Investing time and energy in succession planning and recruiting of others to continue to build on your legacy, thinking ahead to the time when you will be ready to hand your work off.

- Developing outside interests and hobbies that bring meaning and fulfillment, both for their own innate value and for the sake of arriving at your Capstone phase with pursuits to explore beyond your work.

- Mentoring early and mid-career professionals about individual contributor and leadership roles and beginning to share with them your learnings about the process of Intentional Career Design.

How Do I Know I Am Ready to Move to the Next Career Stage?

As a coach, I know someone is wrapping up the Independent Professional stage when they start saying things like, "I have someone I am preparing to take over my leadership role," or "My spouse is asking me to think about buying a retirement home," or "I had a friend who died too young, and I'm beginning to think about what else I want to do with my life beyond work." When I hear comments like these, I know my clients may be ready to step fully out of frontline contribution roles and move toward full-time administration or leadership, and their organizations may be ready for them to do so as well.

Folks who have completed this work have clarity about the next steps in their career, who will take over the parts of their work that can and should continue, and who will take over their various roles as they become ready to shed them. They are making plans with their personal stakeholders for a life beyond work, and they are generally satisfied with their progress to date. If this sounds familiar, you may be in this stage too.

Strategies for Success

Self-Care Strategies

Our standard self-care recommendations apply here, but there is an important additional strategy worth considering. Many professionals arrive at this point in their career harboring a good bit of trepidation about what comes next and what gives their life meaning. I encourage you, if you are struggling with concerns about facing retirement, existential questions related to peers and friends passing away early, or other similar worries, to consider this. Whether you have a spiritual practice that brings you meaning or not, seek a trusted advisor in your faith tradition, or connect with a professional coach or counselor who can help you explore the ideas of meaning and purpose. Consolidating your understanding of those things is an essential step in your senior career phase and beyond.

Intentional Career Design Strategies

Even at a time that you may feel crystal clear on your priorities, it's helpful to maintain your habit of keeping your Top Ten List of what matters most to you up to date. I'll also suggest an exercise that may help you think about that question of meaning and purpose. Some coaches ask clients to write their own eulogy, but I prefer a different approach. I ask my clients to write the retirement speech that they hope *someone else* gives about them when they reach that point. I ask them to summarize the key accomplishments and describe the key steps that occurred between today and that fictitious future retirement celebration. What did they accomplish, and how exactly did they go about doing it? What were their overarching priorities and values that allowed those accomplishments? Are they excited about what comes next, and why? And what advice would they share with a person just entering the mid-career stage? This is called a "History of the Future" exercise, and it can be powerful. If you do write such a document, place it in a sealed envelope and arrange to have it delivered to you at the time of your retirement.

Other Tips

Once again, this is a good time to consult with financial and legal advisors, as well as spiritual advisors if appropriate for you. It's also time to be sure you are up-to-date on preventive health screenings, and that you set aside time to have deepening conversations with those closest to you about your hopes and dreams for the next stage of your life and your career. Talk to them. Listen to them. They will have wisdom and insight, and maybe some great advice.

CHAPTER 19 – SUMMARY

The Independent Professional stage of mid-career is noted for clarity of purpose and effort, and a focus that is turning toward legacy and the future, including life beyond work. It is a time to consolidate your professional reputation and begin to plan for the next stage of life and career.

Core Concepts

- The Independent Professional Stage begins with a notable shift to clarity of purpose, recognition of success at the external level, and a focus on active steps to support succession planning. Mid-level to senior leadership roles may come at this time.

- Key Developmental Tasks in this stage include developing and securing your professional reputation, succeeding at leadership roles if accepted, focusing on active steps to plan for continuation of work that will outlast you in your role and mentoring of those behind you on the journey.

- Strategies for Success in this stage include the ever-present self-care tactics, including working with a trusted spiritual or secular advisor to explore what gives meaning and purpose to your life.

- Intentional Career Design steps for this stage include maintaining a current Top Ten List of what matters most to you, and writing a History of the Future document, then arranging to have someone deliver it to you at your transition to the Capstone phase of your career.

Key Takeaways

What are your Key Takeaways from this chapter? What did you learn, in your own words?

Very Next Actions

After reading this chapter, are there any Very Next Actions (VNAs) you need to take based on what you have learned?

VNA #1:

VNA #2:

Senior Career Part 1 – Recognized Expert

I f you have arrived at the Recognized Expert Stage of your senior career, you are known for your professional successes, both within your organization and beyond. You are probably saying the "strategic yes" to fewer things, typically only those that hold significant meaning for you. You are getting much more comfortable with the idea of saying the "strategic no." You will have begun to plan and implement action steps to support your legacy for both your professional individual contributions and your administrative and leadership work. You continue to publicly disseminate your work and are increasingly recognized for significant accomplishments. Your reputation within and beyond your organization has been secured.

You may be considering alternatives to traditional career paths, and opportunities you did not expect may present themselves. Curveballs, both positive and challenging, appear with more frequency. In this stage, you may be actively thinking about an encore career or retirement, or perhaps considering how you will stay active and engaged in work until you are ready to stop working. This may be a frightening time, particularly if you have not been intentional about planning for this stage. It may be even harder if you do not have hobbies, activities, or interests beyond work that bring you joy and fulfillment. You should know, though, that it's never too late to bring intention to this process. If you are reading this book, it will have just what you need to bring your attention to this stage of your career.

Developmental Tasks

- Developmental tasks in this stage focus on taking stock of success and planning for what's next. Specific tasks include planning for completion of your professional endeavors. Is there work still to be done that you feel strongly about completing yourself? This is a perfect time to focus on that. And will there be work to be done when you step away? If yes, determine who will take it over and whether you can or should step back at some point to allow that person or team to move forward without you?

- Reviewing new opportunities—is there something new you want to take on? A new role, a new project, one that holds your passion and enthusiasm or something you have always wanted to do? This may be the time to seek out that kind of opportunity.

- Mentoring of those behind you on the journey will continue, and you have increasingly more wisdom you can share about your work, organizations, and their systems, and even about this process of intentionally designing your work. Your mentees will be grateful.

- Consideration of your options for the Capstone portion of your career. This is the time to think about what you might want to do next, when your current career path is complete. You may be hoping to retire and garden or travel, or you may be planning a second career or to devote yourself to work with a not-for-profit organization. The point now is to be thinking about it and putting things in place that will allow you to move seamlessly to that plan when you are ready.

How Do I Know I Am Ready to Move to the Next Career Stage?

Moving from the Recognized Expert stage to the next stage is sometimes a gradual change that is not readily apparent. It can sneak up on you. You will notice that you are more focused on that big project you always wanted to do; you may have stepped out of all your individual contributor work to focus on administrative or leadership activities. You are being asked to mentor several people, while you may field requests for meetings to share your wisdom. Your plans for your Capstone stage are coming into focus, and you are doing what's needed to make that a smooth transition.

Strategies for Success

Self-Care Strategies

Self-care continues to be important, in all the ways it has been throughout this journey. One tip for self-care that may not seem apparent is that it's OK to take time to just do nothing. This was true all along, but your entire career has likely been task-oriented, so you may have difficulty pressing pause to just be still. Allowing yourself time to daydream, think, or just sit and enjoy a cup of coffee with a friend is a wonderful and necessary gift. I call this "hopping off the treadmill" and it's a valuable habit that is particularly helpful as you are consolidating everything you have learned. Your brain is wired to use these periods of rest to integrate your emotions, knowledge, hopes, and dreams. If you've never done this, try it out now—give yourself permission for "daydream breaks," at least weekly if not more often.

Intentional Career Design Strategies

You will find that the Top Ten List of what matters most to you gets easier to update, but the things that are important to you are likely shifting. This is a fantastic reason to keep it up to date. The other strategy I like to suggest in this stage is a planning exercise. Using pen and paper or the electronic device of your choice, make a Capstone Roadmap or step-by-step plan outlining how you want the year before you step away from this career to go. With whom will you need to talk? What do you need to do to pursue that second career? Do you need to choose and buy a vacation home, practice your fly-fishing, or take a Master Gardener class? Write out that plan and a timeline to go with it. You're not ready to step away yet, but having a plan for the process will help relieve some of your anxiety about it and will help you prepare to do the things you want to do.

Other Tips

This may be no surprise by now, but I think consulting with your legal and financial planning team is a must in this period. It's time to clue them in on what you want to do in your Capstone phase, if you haven't already done so, and it's also time to talk with significant others (spouse and children) about what you want this stage of life to look like. Hopefully, you are already doing this, but if not, you really must start now. Senior career and beyond is not the time to keep it all to yourself. Of course, you'll want to listen to their thoughts as well. You all have a lot to look forward to.

CHAPTER 20 – SUMMARY

This stage can be a lot of fun—your reputation is secure, you are focusing on work that you choose to do, and you are crafting your plan for what comes next. Take time to enjoy it, and to pause to savor it.

Core Concepts

- The Senior Expert stage begins when you understand that your reputation is secure, you still have work you want to do, and you are in a place where you can choose where to focus your time and energy.

- Key Developmental Tasks in this stage include planning for completion of the work you want to do, making a succession plan to hand off the work you want to continue, reviewing any new opportunities that bring you energy and enthusiasm, continuing to mentor others, and beginning to make a concrete plan for the Capstone phase.

- Strategies for Success in this stage include continuing to practice good self-care strategies, allowing time to daydream or otherwise pause and enjoy things around you, and beginning to discuss concrete plans for what's next with your significant others and with your team of financial and legal advisors as needed.

- Intentional Career Design steps for this stage include keeping that Top Ten List of what matters most to you current and creating a Capstone Roadmap with concrete steps to help you get ready for the things you want to do going forward.

Key Takeaways

What are your Key Takeaways from this chapter? What did you learn, in your own words?

Very Next Actions

After reading this chapter, are there any Very Next Actions (VNAs) you need to take based on what you have learned?

VNA #1:

VNA #2:

Senior Career Part 2 – Wise Elder

Wise Elder may sound like a pretentious title, and that may not be how you think of yourself at this stage, but it's how others see you. You may not formally be an "elder," but in your profession and in your organization, you've been around for a while, and you know how things work. You understand the magic that happens behind the curtain, and you know how the sausage is made, so to speak. That's valuable knowledge. You have accomplished most of what you wanted to do, though you may still have some things you want to wrap up. You have a plan for how you want things to go in the coming years, and you are implementing it, both at work and in your personal life. People come to you for advice and wisdom—professionally, politically, and personally. You may find that you are given a lot of deference, or you may find that you are not and that is challenging. Either way, you have the chance to wrap things up and make a concrete plan for making your next move.

Developmental Tasks

This stage is a time of completion and planning to move forward. Specific tasks to be accomplished include:

- Continuing to contribute professionally and administratively to the projects and parts of your work that you enjoy. This is the time to use all that you know to move the work forward in ways you can celebrate.

- Mentoring those who are coming behind you can be a deeply rewarding part of this phase. It may even seem like that is your primary work at this point, and that's more than acceptable. It can be fun to know that you are continuing to build your legacy in this way, and you are probably mentoring those who are most critical to your succession planning.

- Considering the right time to move to Capstone. You may wonder, "How do I know if I have stayed too long?" or "When is the right time to go?" There is no easy or singular answer to this question, but it's time to assess your energy and enthusiasm for continuing to work, as well as the organization's energy or enthusiasm for you staying. When either of those seem to be waning, it's a good time to start putting your plans into motion.

- Graciously accepting public recognition of significant accomplishments. You are at a point where major awards and other forms of recognition may begin to happen, and it's OK to enjoy that.

- Begin implementing the concrete steps on your Capstone Roadmap. It's time to start thinking about the administrative tasks that will need to be done to make a transition.

How Do I Know I Am Ready to Move to the Next Career Stage?

Knowing when the time is ripe to implement your Capstone Plan can seem like a fraught question. It really comes down to how you want to manage your time and energy. Are you still enthusiastic about the professional work you are doing? Is there still work to be done? Do you have your Capstone Plans in place, or are you still working on them? When your energy and enthusiasm for what's next outweighs your energy and enthusiasm for what you are doing, it's time to move forward!

Strategies for Success

Self-Care Strategies

Routine self-care is critical in this stage, as always, so continue to pay attention. In case you've forgotten my list of basic self-care tips, I'll share it here again:

- A good physical self-care routine that includes exercise, sleep, and healthy nutrition.
- A network of family, friends, and confidants with whom to talk about what is happening as you move through this stage.
- A spiritual source of support if that is important to you.
- A mental health support system if appropriate.

Intentional Career Design Strategies

Update your Top Ten List of what matters most to you and ask yourself what is changing or transitioning right now. This tool is useful for assessing where your personal energy is focused. Take some time to review your Capstone Roadmap and do the Energy Assessment portion of this document to help you determine timing for the next phase.

Other Tips

Continue to have conversations with those closest to you about how they see your energy and enthusiasm, what they are worried about, and what they hope to see for you and for themselves as you plan your Capstone transition. These people have always been valuable sounding boards, and that is never more true than at this stage. Talk with and listen to them.

An important note: It's OK to focus on the work you have enthusiasm for—this stage is not all about planning to step away. From a psychological development standpoint, moving into the Capstone phase provokes a good bit of anxiety for some people and a lot of enthusiasm for others. If you're unsure, know that you can hang out in this stage for a while and enjoy it. Just pay attention to whether and how the energy is shifting for you, those closest to you, and your organization. When the net energy and enthusiasm points to staying, then stay. When it points to moving forward, you'll know what to do.

CHAPTER 21 – SUMMARY

This is a stage of consolidation, celebration of accomplishments, and shifting energies. Pay attention to what holds your energy and enthusiasm, enjoy the chance to do what you love most, and decide when it's time to move forward from here.

Core Concepts

- The Wise Elder Stage begins when you and others around you recognize that you have wisdom to share, and this becomes a major focus of your daily work. Mentoring others and working on meaningful contributions that move your field forward are key parts of this stage.

- Key Developmental Tasks in this stage include continuing to contribute to your professional, administrative, or leadership work as long as you have enthusiasm for doing so, mentoring others (this may take more of your time than you expected) and assessing your energy and that of those around you to determine when to implement your Capstone Roadmap plans.

- Strategies for Success in this stage include the standard self-care strategies and continued conversations with those in your personal life who will be most affected by your timing and next steps.

- Intentional Career Design steps for this stage include keeping your Top Ten List of what matters most to you up to date and reviewing the Energy Assessment portion of your Capstone Roadmap to help you know when you are ready to implement your Capstone plan.

Key Takeaways

What are your Key Takeaways from this chapter? What did you learn, in your own words?

Very Next Actions

After reading this chapter, are there any Very Next Actions (VNAs) you need to take based on what you have learned?

VNA #1:

VNA #2:

Capstone Phase –
Transitioning to the Next Adventure

S o, what is this Capstone thing we've been hinting at and building up to? Well, it's not what you think. It may come at the end of a long career, but it may alternatively come sooner than you think. You don't have to be "of a certain age" to get here, and it's not necessarily the last thing you will do as a professional. It is a little hard to do after just a few years in the work world, but I have met what I call "serial professionals" who cycle through three, four, or even more careers, and who move through all the career stages rapidly, then get to this point and reinvent themselves.

I invite you to consider the Capstone as a time when you are ready to close one chapter of your work life and move to another. You might think it's all about retirement, but it's not. The Capstone is just what its name implies— the pinnacle and point of closure for one cycle of your work life. What's next depends on you and what matters most to you. Your next step may be an Encore Career, the next professional thing you want to do. You may need to get formal training, a new degree, or some experience in a new field in order to pursue an Encore, but it's something new that could have energy and life for you for a season, and it's a reinvention of your professional self and of your relationship with work.

It is also possible that your Encore Career will keep you in the same field, but in a more altruistic way that may mean less compensation but more autonomy and a larger chance to give back to others. You may not need more training to take this approach, but you do generally need some financial security to undertake a change of this magnitude.

Alternatively, you may be ready to completely retire from the world of professional work. Retirement is not the same as an Encore Career—it really means that you're going to stop working, but a rich and fulfilling life can continue. Retirement means different things to different people. It may be a time to travel; it may be time to focus on your home and garden, and to "nest" in a way you have never had opportunity to do. And it may be a time to pursue recreation in a new way—devoting the time and energy to learn and practice fly-fishing, for example.

What retirement usually ***doesn't*** mean is taking to a rocking chair and sitting on the front porch day after day (although that sounds just lovely for some days). What matters is that you have autonomy to choose.

All these choices require prior planning. That's why I asked you to start thinking about the Capstone Roadmap from the very beginning of our journey through the Life Course of a Career. These choices also assume that you have reasonable health and some financial security. That is not the case for everyone, and no matter how much prior planning you do, sometimes life throws you a curveball that interferes with what you thought you would be able to do in this phase. In the face of curveballs, you can fall back on your Top Ten List of what matters most to you and say, "What has been most important to me? How much of my original plan am I able to achieve or do given the curveball I am facing?" Revise your list based on your circumstances, then go after those things that are possible.

The point of this stage is that with luck and forward planning, you have choices to make rather than a list of "metrics for success." The metrics become internal, driven by your values—your own compass. If you are a serial professional starting on a new Encore Career, enjoy the ride, and monitor where you are in the life course of your new career. This model holds up if you choose a new path, no matter how many times you repeat the process.

Developmental Tasks

Key Developmental Tasks in this stage really are driven by what you choose to do. They may include:

- Planning your offboarding from one career and onboarding into another or into retirement (see chapter 11—the onboarding and offboarding strategies still apply)

- Figuring out what to do with your time if you are not going to work every day.

- Developing hobbies, passions, and activities that bring you joy, meaning, and purpose beyond your work identity.

- Being gentle with yourself if the first part of the transition is a bit rocky.

- Communicating clearly with those around you who may or may not recognize what is happening for you and who have their own responses to your transition. Keep talking and keep listening.

What's Next?

You might think that your professional journey is complete. It may be if you have chosen a retirement pathway. Alternatively, you may be a serial professional who is planning and implementing your Encore Career. It is also possible you will try retirement and then decide you want an Encore, or vice versa. It's a period of life and work in which you get to make the choice every day.

Strategies for Success

Self-Care Strategies

Practicing self-care in ways that maintain your current level of health or even enhance it will allow you more freedom of choice in this stage, so keep focusing on all the self-care steps I've described. In addition, keep talking with and listening to those around you about how things are going—what are your needs, and what are theirs during this transition?

Intentional Career Design Strategies

This is a time to keep up with your Top Ten List of what matters most to you and to use all the other steps of Intentional Career Design that you have learned to help you make decisions as you move through this stage. There are no new tools to complete, just lessons learned and a habit of making intentional decisions about how you want to spend your time and energy.

Other Tips

At this point, my other important tip is to have some fun. You've made a journey—it may be over many years, and it may be shorter. You have completed a cycle of growth and meaning. Celebrate it, enjoy the fruits of the work you have done, and keep focusing on those things that give you meaning, purpose, and joy. That's why it is critical to keep identifying and refining what matters most to you.

CHAPTER 22 – SUMMARY

The Capstone phase can be exhilarating, exciting, and anxiety-provoking—all at the same time. You may have one Capstone in your lifetime, or many. It doesn't matter. Take stock, celebrate, and make choices that allow you to maximize your sense of meaning, purpose, and joy.

Core Concepts

- The Capstone stage begins when you are ready to close one cycle of your work life and move to another. It may come at the end of a long career in a single profession, or you may be a serial professional who moves through two, three, or more Encore Careers over your lifetime. This phase is one of completion—and renewal.

- Key Developmental Tasks in this stage include planning your transition strategies, figuring out how you want to spend your time, developing hobbies, passions, and routines that are meaningful to you, and being gentle with yourself about the transition.

- Strategies for Success in this stage include continuing to practice good self-care habits and communicating well with those around you about how the transition is going—for you and for them. It's also worth making time and space to celebrate the completion of your professional journey—even if you have another one planned.

- Intentional Career Design strategies for this stage include keeping your Top Ten List of what matters most to you up to date and using all the Intentional Career Design techniques you have learned along the way. Opportunities and choices will continue to emerge for you. Fortunately, you are well prepared to manage those opportunities and choices in a way that works for you and those you care about.

Key Takeaways

What are your Key Takeaways from this chapter? What did you learn, in your own words?

Very Next Actions

After reading this chapter, are there any Very Next Actions (VNAs) you need to take based on what you have learned?

VNA #1:

VNA #2:

PART 5:

Putting it All Together

Congratulations! Hopefully by now you understand that bringing an intentional approach to your career design means you really can build a meaningful and satisfying professional career that gets you where you want to go, while also leaving time and space for a rich and fulfilling personal life.

Now, to ensure you are fully prepared to bring these ideas to your own life, I want to share a concept that will consolidate them and provide you with that professional road map we have been talking about. I call it a Career Design Plan, and it uses all the elements you have learned about in this book. The Career Design Plan is an iterative document that you can begin at any point in your career. It's also intended to be dynamic and grow with you as you learn about yourself and those you care about, as you discover what matters most to you and your stakeholders and as your life circumstances evolve.

Take a bit of time to think about what you have learned, then put it all together. It's just what you need for that intentionally designed career we have been discussing—and the Bespoke Life it will allow you to create.

Building and Maintaining Your Career Design Plan

A Review of the Core Elements of Professional Careers by Design

Creating a Career Design Plan is made possible by the work you have done already, using strategies of Professional Careers by Design™ that we have been talking about throughout this book. The tools and tips you have learned here come together in three major elements.

- The Discernment Process: Using the Five Steps of Intentional Career Design and tips for managing curveballs to stay current in your understanding of what matters most to you and to those you care about. Remember that important quote from my mentor, "Work and home, it's all one life." What matters most to you is not just a question about your work life.

- The Career Transitions Cycle: A roadmap for use when you are in an active career transition or are considering making such a shift.

- Lifelong Context: Developing a Capstone Plan and using the Life Course of a Career phases and stages to understand your level of professional development and where you want to go next.

Dynamic Career Planning Strategies for a Lifetime

Here's a way to think about when and how (and how often) to use these tools over the course of your working lifetime. I offer this as a both a road-map and a tool to guide your use of the material I've shared with you in this book over the course of your lifetime.

- Annually or whenever your life circumstances change:
  - Update your Top Ten List of what matters most to you and ask your stakeholders to update their lists as well.
  - Review your stakeholders' lists and compare notes with each of them.
  - Review and update your Capstone Plan—even if you are early in your career.

- Whenever a curveball comes up—good or bad:
  - Revisit your Top Ten List of what matters most to you and ask your stakeholders to do the same.
  - Assess what you are getting from your work life in terms of the Four Es—what does that tell you about staying or going?
  - Assess your need to stay or go, using the Stay/Go Grid.

- Whenever you decide that it is time to look for another role, job, or organization:
  - Continue to update your Top Ten List of what matters most to you.
  - Review and determine where you are in the Career Transitions Cycle.
  - Work through the steps for your stage of the Career Transitions Cycle.

- Make the best decision you can with the information you have.

- Whenever you are questioning the long-term trajectory of your career:
  - Review your Top Ten List of what matters most to you.
  - Review the phases and stages of the Life Course of a Career.
  - Ask yourself if your Capstone Plan is up-to-date, and if not, what might need to change.
  - Ask yourself where you fall in the Life Course of a Career. Are you moving into a new career stage? What developmental tasks are next for you, and how will you ensure that you thrive through this period of your professional growth?

Don't forget, as I have mentioned earlier in this book, having a close friend, spouse, partner, or other person you trust and who is willing to listen as you explore all these questions will be helpful. The other critically important thing to remember about all of this is that the work of an intentionally designed career does not end when you land your dream job, nor even when you retire (*if* you retire), nor are these principles limited to the professional areas of your life. If you choose to be intentional, there will always be work and reflection to be done. That is why for many of my clients, Intentional Career Design is just the beginning of building what I call a Bespoke Life. A life that in all its aspects (professional, spiritual, physical, intellectual, and every other aspect of which you can imagine) serves what matters most to you and those you care most about. As you make these processes habits, I invite you to consider how you could apply them broadly to craft an entire life that is uniquely yours and uniquely meaningful.

Thank you for taking this journey with me, and I wish for you a satisfying, exciting, and fulfilling pathway to an intentionally designed career that is an anchor point of your Bespoke Life.

CHAPTER 23 TOOL

Purpose

No matter where you are in the process, this checklist will help you identify immediate steps you can take using the Professional Careers by Design(TM) model.

Instructions

Whenever you are facing a career decision, or during your annual planning process, assess where you are in the process of lifetime career design and complete the items relevant to that part of the checklist. Revisit the checklist often.

Annually or whenever your life circumstances change:

☐ Update your Top Ten List of what matters most to you, and ask your stakeholders to update their lists as well.

☐ Review your stakeholders' lists, and compare notes with each of them.

☐ Review and update your Capstone Plan – even if you are early in your career.

Whenever a curveball comes up – good or bad:

☐ Revisit and review your Top Ten List of what matters most to you, and ask your stakeholders to do the same.

☐ Assess which of the Four E's you are getting from your work life – what does that tell you about staying or going?

☐ Assess your need to stay or go, using the Stay/Go Grid.

Whenever you decide that it is time to look for another role, job, or organization:

☐ Continue to update your Top Ten List of what matters most to you.

☐ Review and determine where you are in the Career Transitions Cycle.

☐ Work through the steps for your stage of the Career Transitions Cycle.

☐ Make the best decision you can with the information you have.

Lifetime Career Design Checklist
Page 2

Whenever you are questioning the long-term trajectory of your career:

☐ Review your Top Ten List of what matters most to you.

☐ Review the phases and stages of the Life Course of a Career and determine your current stage.

☐ Ask yourself if your Capstone plan is up to date, and if not, what might need to change.

☐ Ask yourself what's next for you in the Life Course of a Career. Are you moving into a new career stage? What developmental tasks are next for you, and how will you ensure you thrive through this period of your professional growth?

Add your own questions here:

☐

☐

☐

☐

☐

And don't forget, having a close friend, spouse, partner, or other person you trust and who is willing to listen as you explore all of these questions will be helpful.

CHAPTER 23 – SUMMARY

A Career Design Checklist is the culmination of the work of the Professional Careers by Design™ methodology. Using this checklist to create your real-time career plan, updating the checklist and the plan regularly, and having a repeatable process that you trust yourself to complete will allow you to respond to career challenges over the course of your lifetime, manage specific changes you need to make, and ground yourself in the things that matter most to you.

Core Concepts

- A Career Design Plan is both a document and a process. It's a repeatable series of questions and steps to be taken at regular intervals throughout your career. It builds on all the components of Professional Careers by Design™ and asks you to reiterate the process as often as needed.

- Key components of the Career Design Plan include:

  - The Discernment Process: Outcomes of your explorations

  - The Career Transitions Cycle: Key steps for managing a career transition

  - Lifelong Context: Taking perspective of your career over an extended period of time

Key Takeaways

What are your Key Takeaways from this chapter? What did you learn, in your own words?

Very Next Actions

After reading this chapter, are there any Very Next Actions (VNAs) you need to take based on what you have learned?

VNA #1:

VNA #2:

24

The End and The Beginning

As you come to the conclusion of this book, I encourage you to think of it as both an ending and a beginning. You have explored the three components of the Professional Careers by Design™ approach to intentionally design the career and the life that you want. You have tools and materials to think about and utilize in your own journey. And ... it is truly the beginning. The beginning of that journey to creating an intentionally designed life with meaning and purpose that creates good in the world—A Bespoke Life.

I want to invite you to join the free online community exploring this work together. I call it *The Bespoke Life Book Club*, and you may join for free using this QR Code.

Figure 1: QR Code to Enroll in Bespoke Life Book Club

If you join the Bespoke Life Book Club, you will become a member of my larger community, the Bespoke Life Network. Joining the Book Club and Network is free, and signing up will add you to my mailing list and give you access to other benefits of free membership, including:

- **your own copies of the tools we use in this book—in a fillable PDF form for convenient use and reuse, including any updates we make as the needs of our community evolve.**

- Occasional new tools that we design, as well as many other resources that can enhance your exploration of the Professional Careers by Design™ model.

- Opportunities to connect with and learn alongside others who are on a similar journey.

- A purpose-built community created to help you design a Bespoke Life that realizes the meaning and fulfillment you seek.

- Access to additional learning and connection that will help you grow further in myriad directions—from improving your time management to reinforcing critical leadership skills. These include free and premium opportunities such as group and individual coaching, online courses you can complete at your own pace, and live workshops and webinars.

Thank you so much for your interest in this approach to planning your professional and personal life. Remember that your life energy is finite (at least this time around, depending on your belief system) and that "personal and professional—it's all one life," as my friend Lois has said. It's up to you to decide how you want to spend your life energy in the world. I hope this book will help you make the choices that bring you meaning, purpose, peace, and fulfillment.

Once again, I offer you blessings for the journey.

RECOMMENDED ADDITIONAL READING

These books have informed my coaching practice and the guidance in this book over many years. I feel very comfortable recommending them to you as additional tools and resources for your journey to creating a Bespoke Life.

Allen, David. *Getting Things Done: The Art of Stress-Free Productivity.* Revised edition. New York, NY: Penguin Books, 2015.

Babcock, Linda, and Sara Laschever. *Women Don't Ask: Negotiation and the Gender Divide.* Princeton, NJ: Princeton University Press, 2003.

Babcock, Linda, Sara Laschever, and Iris Bohnet. *Women Don't Ask: Negotiation and the Gender Divide.* New paperback ed. Princeton, NJ: Princeton University Press, 2021.

Bateson, Mary Catherine. *Composing a Life.* New York, NY: Grove Press, 2001.

Bateson, Mary Catherine. *Composing a Further Life: The Age of Active Wisdom.* 1st ed. New York, NY: Alfred A. Knopf, 2010.

Borysenko, Joan. *A Woman's Book of Life: The Biology, Psychology, and Spirituality of the Feminine Life Cycle.* New York, NY: The Berkley Publishing Group, 1996.

Brown, Brené. *Rising Strong.* First ed. New York, NY: Spiegel & Grau, 2015.

Brown, C. Brené. *Daring Greatly: How the Courage to Be Vulnerable Transforms the Way We Live, Love, Parent, and Lead.* 1st ed. New York, NY: Gotham Books, 2012.

Burnett, Bill, and Dave Evans. *Designing Your Life: How to Build a Well-Lived, Joyful Life.* New York, NY: Alfred A. Knopf, 2016.

Christensen, Clayton M., James Allworth, and Karen Dillon. *How Will You Measure Your Life?* 1st ed. New York, NY: Harper Business, 2012.

Clark, Dorie. *Reinventing You: Define Your Brand, Imagine Your Future.* Boston, MA: Harvard Business Review Press, 2017

Clark, Dorie. *The Long Game: How to Be a Long-Term Thinker in a Short-Term World.* Boston, MA: Harvard Business Review Press, 2021.

Covey, Stephen R. *The 7 Habits of Highly Effective People.* New York, NY: Simon & Schuster, 2020.

Fisher, Roger, William Ury, and Bruce Patton. Getting to Yes: *Negotiating Agreement without Giving In.* 3rd ed. New York, NY: Penguin, 2011.

Friedman, Stewart D. *Total Leadership: Be a Better Leader, Have a Richer Life.* Boston, MA: Harvard Business Review Press, 2014.

Harris, La'Wana. *Diversity Beyond Lip Service: A Coaching Guide for Challenging Bias.* First ed. Oakland, CA: Berrett-Koehler Publishers, Inc., 2019.

Kendi, Ibram X. *How to Be an Antiracist.* Trade paperback edition. New York, NY: One World, 2023.

Launiere, Beth, and Leo Hopf. *Stop Competing and Start Winning: The Business of Coaching.* 1st ed. Salt Lake City, UT: Mastery Publishing, 2020.

Levine, Suzanne Braun. *Inventing the Rest of Our Lives: Women in Second Adulthood.* New York, NY: Viking, 2005.

Pressfield, Steven. *The War of Art: Break Through the Blocks and Win Your Inner Creative Battles*. New York, NY: Warner Books, 2002.

Pressfield, Steven. *Turning Pro: Tap Your Inner Power and Create Your Life's Work*. New York, NY: Black Irish Entertainment, 2012.

Ury, William. *Getting Past No: Negotiating in Difficult Situations*. Rev. ed. New York, NY: Bantam Books, 2007.

Voss, Chris. *Never Split the Difference: Negotiating as If Your Life Depended on It*. 1st ed. New York, NY: Harper Business, an imprint of Harper Collins Publishers, 2016.

Watkins, Michael. *The First 90 Days: Proven Strategies for Getting up to Speed Faster and Smarter*. Boston, MA: Harvard Business Review Press, 2013.

ABOUT THE AUTHOR

Sharon Hull is a retired family physician also trained in preventive medicine and public health. She has been a professional executive coach for many years and is committed to professional coaching as her second healing profession. She lives in North Carolina with her family, enjoys walking outside in the many beautiful areas of that state, and tends a beautiful garden that gives her many hours of joy.